30-Something and Over It

KASEY EDWARDS

30

Something and Over it

What happens when you get up and don't want to go to work . . . Ever again.

MAINSTREAM
PUBLISHING

EDINBURGH AND LONDON

First published in Great Britain in 2009 by
MAINSTREAM PUBLISHING COMPANY
(EDINBURGH) LTD
7 Albany Street
Edinburgh EH1 3UG

ISBN 9781845964467

This book is substantially a work of non-fiction based on the life experiences and
recollections of the author. In some limited cases, names and descriptions of people,
places and the detail of events have been changed for artistic purposes and to protect
the privacy of others.

All illustrations by Gill McColl

A catalogue record for this book is available
from the British Library.

Typeset in Garamond and Hombre

Printed and bound by
CPI Group (UK) Ltd, Croydon, CR0 4YY

To my lovely Christopher, who enriches me in so many ways.
I can write a whole book, but I simply don't have the words
to express what you mean to me.

✳

When you've gained everything you knew for certain you'd always wanted, you'd think living happily ever after would be the easy part. Obviously, it's time to think again.

Susan Maushart,
What Women Want Next

ACKNOWLEDGEMENTS

This journey started one Sunday night when I was sharing curry and a bottle of wine with Christopher Scanlon, Emma Lindsay and Michael Edwards. They inspired me, challenged me and encouraged me from the very beginning and through every crisis in confidence along the way. Thank you for holding my hand on this journey, for your unwavering love and support, and for your brilliant editing. Thank you to Jackie Yowell for your encouragement and editorial and industry advice; to Jules Cole, who helped me fix the boring bits and 'fabulized' me with her brilliant photography; to Brandy Walton for having the courage to tell me what didn't work; and to my mum Jan Edwards, who proofread the manuscript to within an inch of its life.

Thank you to my friends and colleagues who cheered me on, shared their wisdom and didn't complain when I bored them senseless with every detail. It would have been much harder without you: Ann Marie Abinoja, Madlen Altstaedt, Sarea Coates, Fiona Coote, Wylie Easthope, Stephen Farquhar, Dean Grandy, Pierre-Francis Grillet, Michelle Hendrie, Gerard Koelmeyer, Rebecca Lowth, Nadia Michaelides, Jacki O'Mara, Micheal Papasava, Sven Peters and Troy Townsend. Many thanks also to Kathy Lette for your encouragement and endorsement of my book.

This book would have been very short indeed if it weren't for all the people who graciously shared their stories and insights with me. Thank you to: Godfrey Boyd, Caroline Cameron, Kate Edwards, Nigel Marsh, Susan Maushart, Melissa McLean, Jamie Rossato, Rachel Sheehan and all the other people whose names I've changed to protect their privacy. You know who you are.

Many thanks to my agents Jane Graham Maw and Jennifer Christie, who plucked me from obscurity and sold my book to the wonderful people at Mainstream who championed it from the start: Ailsa Bathgate, Fiona Brownlee, Bill Campbell and Emily Bland.

Finally, thank you to Adrian Kayman and all the staff at Feedings@ Readings who allowed me to write this book in his café and for making my soy cappuccino just the way I like it.

CONTENTS

WINTER

SPRING

SUGGESTIONS FOR FURTHER READING

INTRODUCTION

Losing my give-a-shit

Have you ever woken up and realised that you didn't want to go to work?

I don't mean you had a big night and wanted to sleep in, or you've got a boring day of meetings ahead of you that you can't be bothered sitting through, or you'd just prefer to take your dog to the park instead. I'm not talking about mild discontent either. I'm talking about being over it – completely and utterly over it.

I don't know how it happened. I didn't see it coming, but almost overnight I didn't want to go to work any more – not just on that day, but ever again.

This was a shocking revelation for me. I'd always been one of those ambitious over-achievers with something to prove. For the last ten years, I'd slavishly climbed the corporate ladder, loving every rung of it. I'd kept every business card from every job I'd ever had as scalps of my conquests, with my latest card carrying the title of 'Senior Change Management Consultant'. As a change manager, I spent my days advising clients on how to make their employees more efficient and compliant. The prefix of 'senior' on my business card meant that sometimes the clients even listened to my advice. But I suddenly realised that the ladder that had seemed so important to climb wasn't leading *to* anywhere; it was just taking me further away from where I had started.

I had everything I'd always wanted – a successful career and the lifestyle and assets to match. But all of a sudden my job didn't seem that challenging or glamorous. The role I'd been playing of high-powered businesswoman felt inauthentic and disingenuous, and my whole lifestyle had lost its zing. I'd lost my reason to get out of bed in the morning, and I felt like I'd lost a part of me along with it.

Right about now would be a good time to accuse me of being a poor little rich girl. What on earth did I have to complain about? I was in my 30s, educated, middle class and white, which was pretty much a passport to whatever I wanted. Sure, I was a woman, and almost as short as Kylie Minogue without the arse to compensate, but other than that all the cards were stacked in my favour.

I know that on the scale of problems such as world hunger and breast cancer, this 30-something crisis, or 'thrisis', doesn't even register. I also know that it was a luxury for me to have been able to even contemplate the concept of job satisfaction when most people in the world have to work just to stay alive. But despite feeling unjustified and indulgent, I was terrified at the prospect of working for the next 30 years in a state of unfulfilled monotony.

I needed to discover why I'd lost my give-a-shit and figure out what I could do to find it again. So over the course of 12 months or so, I read books, spoke to experts, talked to people who were over it and also people who were still into it, as well as dabbling in a whole host of escapist and dysfunctional behaviour. When I started this journey, I feared I was the only one who felt like this. But once I came out of the closet and admitted I was over it, I realised, to my amazement and immense relief, I was far from alone. I was shocked by the number of people who had lost their ambition and sense of meaning in their work but spent their lives pretending that they hadn't. Along the way, I realised that all the things that I had considered difficult in my life, like getting my education, working long hours and climbing the corporate ladder, were in fact relatively easy. The really hard thing was stepping off the treadmill and taking an honest look at myself and my life: asking who I really was and what I really wanted.

I realised that losing my give-a-shit about work was not a failure or anything to feel embarrassed or ashamed of. In fact, being 30-something and over it was actually the next rung on the ladder of life that I needed to climb and conquer.

This is my story about being 30-something and over it. I'm not an expert, and I certainly don't have all the answers, but if you're 30-something and over it and find yourself wondering what it's all about, at the very least I hope this book will help you realise that other people are as fucked up as you.

Summer

'For me, the summer will be pure grey'
– Gianni Versace

1

CURRY AND BONDAGE

'I think you need to be whipped,' my brother Michael says, spooning curry onto his plate.

I am sitting in a cosy Indian restaurant with three of my favourite people on the planet. Michael grins mischievously, my best friend Emma laughs out loud, and my partner Chris chokes on his wine.

I'm not at all surprised or offended that my big brother is recommending I try my hand – or Chris's hand – at S&M. I learned very early in life that I should take everything Michael says with a pinch of salt. I still remember him showing me a cow being milked on *Sesame Street* when I was about five years old. With all the wisdom and worldly authority of a seven year old, he informed me that the milk was coming out of the cow's dick. It wasn't until I discovered Baileys that I started consuming dairy products again.

I don't see Michael very often. He spends his life wandering the globe from one job to the next with no fixed address, so whenever we are in the same city I look forward to his alternative and bizarre perspective on whatever is going on in my life at the time.

Emma and I are telling Michael and Chris about how we both realised, almost simultaneously, that we don't want to work any more. Emma and I have been friends for almost half our lives. She is one cool chick, with an irreverent sense of humour and an unbelievable sense of style. She's also one of the most sought-after marketing experts in town.

We'd caught up for coffee a couple of days earlier and she confessed to me that she was completely over work. When her discontent set in about six months ago, she resigned from her job as marketing manager at a retail organisation and found a new job at a telecommunications company. Four months into her new job, she has realised that the job wasn't the problem. The problem is her.

'You need to be whipped,' Michael continues, reaching for a poppadom, 'because you need to experience a life that is outside the one that was prescribed for you.'

He says that for our entire lives both Emma and I have done exactly what was expected of us. We are over-achieving 'good girls', and now we're bored with it. We've reached the point where we need to live our own lives, not the ones that were set out for us. Apparently whipping will take us outside our comfort zone and will force us to be bold and adventurous.

I have to admit he has a point. You could never describe my life as bold or adventurous. I've done impulsive things like move to Holland on a whim, but I ended up getting a great job in a multinational organisation, which looked fantastic on my CV. Even though it felt it at the time, it wasn't risky either. If it hadn't worked out, I always knew I could just come home.

What I've achieved to date has been like an inheritance. I have followed a path that was dictated by my family and society. I went to university and studied business communication. I landed a job in public relations, moved on to a better job in online communication, then on to an even better job in change management. I acquired my Masters degree in change management along the way and have been working my way up the management consulting ranks. Sure, I worked hard to achieve these things and sometimes the path was rocky and an uphill struggle, but no matter how hard it got, there was always a pre-determined course to follow. I've always done what was expected of me – what my parents wanted, what my teachers wanted, what my bosses wanted. And society supported this path and reinforced my compliance. I was praised and rewarded every time I reached and passed a new milestone.

Until now, I've been too busy ticking off my achievements and progressing along the path to stop to question whether or not this is even the right track for me. I feel as though staring into the face of my inheritance is like contemplating a death sentence, and there is a little voice inside me daring me to quit the highway and go off road: daring me to be whipped.

'The thing is, Kase,' Michael continues, 'you've run out of boxes to tick. You've achieved everything you set out to achieve. You've proved yourself, and now you don't know what to do next. Now you need to set your own course.'

Michael knows a thing or two about setting his own course. He is one of those sickening people who are brilliant at everything – maths, languages, sports, arts. When we were young, he memorised an encyclopaedia just because he could. And to top it all off he is laugh-out-loud funny. Someone this talented would be easy to hate, but he's immensely likeable as well. I hate that.

You would think he could have been anything he wanted in life. However, he'll tell you that wasn't the case – he only has one path in life and that path is music. My parents realised he had talent when he taught himself how to play the keyboard and started playing the music from commercials he'd heard on TV. As an adult, he progressed to composing music for commercials. Now he spends his time writing music for film and for other artists and touring with them.

Michael once told me that music is not what he does, it is who he is. It would be easy to romanticise his alternative life path but it has been hard and at times really lonely for him. I witnessed the ten years of poverty, sacrifice and social disapproval he endured before he starting making a half-decent living. I could never have tolerated the staple diet of baked beans and toast, let alone the constant questioning as to when he was going to stop being silly and get a 'real job'.

I remember one time when he entertained the idea of conforming to society and getting a 'real job'. We went through the employment pages together and discovered there wasn't a lot of demand for somebody with degrees in music, philosophy and theology, and whose only practical work experience consisted of writing and performing music. It was a crushing realisation for Michael that even if he wanted to get a real job it was going to be tough for him.

I've always thought of myself as an over-achiever, but listening to Michael's advice I'm starting to wonder if I am actually behind the curve when it comes to emotional and personal development. How is it that I could have reached my 30s and never before have asked myself those self-defining questions of 'what makes me happy?' and 'what do I want to do with my life?' I've never thought about whether or not I am on the right path for me; all I've focused on was how far and how fast I could progress along it. I can't help but wonder if I could have avoided this crisis if I'd been more self-aware or read more Jean-Paul Sartre, or some other angst-ridden intellectual, in my late teens or early 20s. If I'd had the awareness and the guts to choose my own path back then, would I have got the pain over and done with, or would it have made no difference at all?

The scary thing is that I don't know what makes me happy. I have no idea what I'm supposed to do with my life, and even if I did know I probably couldn't afford to do it. I have a mortgage.

Back in the restaurant, Emma says, 'Doing what you love surely doesn't have to equate to poverty. We have to find something we love doing that also pays the bills.'

Now is a good time to introduce you to Chris. Other than being a stellar boyfriend, Chris is a living, breathing example of somebody who lost his give-a-shit, found his passion and is making money from it.

Chris contacted me via an Internet dating website. I responded to him because he seemed to meet all my criteria for a partner – good politics, educated, loves books, loves pets, non-smoker and has no children. As it turned out, he meets a whole stack of other criteria I didn't even know I had.

We met up in person on the day he resigned from being an academic at a university. A career in academia had always been his goal. It was what he thought he always wanted; however, when he got there he realised it didn't fulfil him. He was stifled by the lack of autonomy and the restrictive culture, so after three years he decided to chuck it in and work two days per week as a corporate editor for a secure income, and three days a week as a freelance writer. He's now writing opinion and feature articles for newspapers and magazines and loving every minute of it.

It's been amazing to watch him go from strength to strength as a freelancer. He's so energised by his work and loves the freedom and autonomy that he now has. He's doing so well that editors are contacting him to request he write for them, and, to top it off, he's making more money now than he was as an academic.

'Maybe you should do some research about your crisis,' Chris says. 'It might help you work it out.'

Emma agrees. 'We need to do something.'

'You should also try whipping,' Michael insists. 'It makes your whole body feel like the tip of a penis.'

2

THE JOKE IS ON ME

Now that I've acknowledged that I don't want to go to work any more, showing up every day is almost unbearable.

Each morning, the desire to stay in bed is so strong I feel like I am being physically restrained, as if a big elastic band is holding me to the bed. Every time I attempt to get up, it pulls me back down onto the pillow. On the mornings when Chris manages to get me up early to go to the gym with him, I come home and jump back into bed or snuggle up on the couch with my dog Toffee and watch television. When I am just about to move off the couch and into the bathroom, I am overwhelmed by the need to watch the next segment on breakfast TV. I simply have to find out how to make the perfect vanilla custard or learn which celebrity has been the latest to accessorise with an orphan from Africa. Some days it is necessary to stay watching until the end of the programme so I can find out the results of the viewer poll on whether or not it's acceptable to breastfeed in public.

Before my 30-something crisis, I would bound into work at 8.15 a.m. Now that I'm over it, 8.15 is about the time I start running my bath. And to top it all off, I won't get out of the bath until I've finished drinking my cup of tea and eating my cereal.

Over the last couple of weeks, my start time slipped to 9 a.m., then to 9.15 and has plateaued at about 9.40. When I arrive at the office, I get myself a coffee and then settle down at my desk at about 10 a.m. to start searching the job websites.

Drifting start times is a sure indication of lack of employee engagement. If I'm ever a line manager, I'll have to remember this. In the meantime, when I bump into people in the lift coming in late I smile conspiratorially just so they know that I know their guilty secret.

Lunch starts early and expands into the afternoon. Gone are the days of grabbing a quick bite to eat at my desk. The highlight of my day is going to the pet shop at lunchtime. I go every day to look at the puppies. It started off being a fun and soothing distraction, watching the little balls of fluff roll around in their cages, yelping at people walking by as if demanding to be taken home. But I began to get attached to them. I gave them all names, and now I worry about the ones on their own getting lonely in their cages. Why is it that pet shops insist on segregating dogs according to their breed? Why can't they all play together in the same cage? It breaks my heart to see the four Maltese terriers, which I've named Julian, Dick, Anne and George, playing happily together in their cage while Timmy, the solitary poodle, sits in his cage all by himself.

Timmy is of particular concern to me. I visit him day after day and watch him grow bigger and bigger. Weeks pass and all the Malteses have been sold and their cage is now occupied by Pomeranians, yet Timmy remains. What happens to puppies that aren't sold? Already, Timmy is starting to grow into his oversized paws and ears. Will anybody want him when he isn't so cute and awkwardly puppyish? The woman in the pet shop assures me they always sell every dog. She says that if a dog isn't selling in one shop they move it to another, where it will eventually get sold. It comforts me to hear this, although if it is true, puppies must be the only product in the world where supply never exceeds demand. How odd that I've never read about this universal law in an economics textbook.

I find myself sitting in meetings obsessing about Timmy. He has been stuck in the cage for seven weeks. Surely his time is running out, to say nothing of the lack of stimulation in the cage. I worry that it could be impairing his development and wonder if customers are allowed to buy toys for the puppies. Despite my worry, it feels good to have something to care about. Usually when I'm bored in meetings I think about sex (women are not so different from men), but my maternal instinct is overpowering all other instincts. I convince myself that the only option is to buy Timmy. Sure, it will be a bit crowded in my tiny two-bedroom flat, and Toffee, my eleven-year-old poodle, will take some time to adjust to having a puppy around, but surely it will be good for her to have some company during the day. Toffee must get lonely because I work such long hours. OK, so I'm not working long hours at the moment, but I might do again some day. The human capacity to rationalise almost anything is truly amazing – so is the capacity to forget. Freud says forgetting is a conscious choice; he may be onto something, because I somehow forget to discuss my purchase with Chris.

When I visit the pet shop, cash in hand, Timmy is gone. I think the worst and panic. Has Timmy grown too big and been quietly taken off to the 'other pet shop'? Seeing my distress, the woman behind the counter (the same one who had enlightened me about the amazing demand/supply relationship for puppies) comes over to tell me that Timmy (who turns out to be a girl) was sold yesterday afternoon. She sees my relief and squeezes my arm. They must get people like me all the time. I am immensely relieved that Timmy is alive. I am also relieved that I've been prevented from being stupid – two dogs in a tiny flat was a really dumb idea. Although, as one worry ends, a new one begins – now there is a little beagle sitting all by himself in the cage where Timmy had been.

Besides my time-keeping, the other thing that has markedly deteriorated at work is my attitude. I just don't care any more. I sit in meetings where people are all fired up, having heated debates, and rather than focusing on the content of the discussion I just sit there thinking they are ridiculous.

Even though I used to get just as passionate and concerned over delays in the project schedule or missing a milestone, for the life of me I now cannot muster any sort of emotional response at all. How can I possibly care about artificial deadlines in a project plan? What will be the consequence of missing a bunch of arbitrary dates that somebody wrote on a whiteboard six months ago? The only consequence is that we'll have to do it later, and, given that most of us will probably have to work until we are aged 65, I figure we have plenty of time.

I feel like all of a sudden I've got The Joke, the one that all my naive, gullible colleagues are missing: the one that makes people stay at the office until midnight and miss their partner's birthday party and their children's school play. I realise that all the stress and effort we put into work is meaningless. Most of the time it doesn't matter if things get done or not, and it almost certainly never matters if it is done by me or somebody else. To quote David Brent from *The Office*: 'Never do today what will become someone else's responsibility tomorrow.'

I decide the world can be divided into two groups of people – those who give a shit and those who don't. I start feeling smugly superior because I've worked it out.

My smugness is a passing phase.

I quickly realise that there is a correlation between giving a shit and work satisfaction. All those people I now view as gullible Company Men and Women seem to be enjoying their jobs a hell of a lot more than I am. They care about what they do each day at work and derive satisfaction from achieving things. I used to feel like that too, in the good old days. Now I just feel demotivated and even a little envious. When my boss punches the air and yells 'Go for gold' as if he is experiencing orgasmic euphoria rather than announcing the half-yearly results, I want to clap and feel excited like everybody else. But I don't. Instead, I feel like the only sane person in the asylum.

Could it be that the joke is actually on me? If I have to show up to work each day, surely it's better to enjoy it?

My demotivation morphs into resentfulness. For the first time in my career, I am acutely aware that I am only working for the money. It seems ridiculous that it has taken me over ten years to figure out that I need to work for money. Because I have always been working for other reasons such as status and career development, the financial necessity of working has never occurred to me. I don't care any more about the project, or my pending performance review, or my next promotion. In fact, other than Chris and the puppies, I hardly care about anything at all. I feel outraged and scandalised that I have to show up each day, so I spend most of the day surfing the net and lamenting the fact that I have to be there. My only motivation for doing anything at all is self-preservation. I procrastinate on everything until such time that if I don't do something I'll look completely incompetent.

You may be wondering how I can keep a job while I am behaving like this. Interestingly enough, in some aspects not giving a shit makes me better at my job.

As a consultant, I often have to deliver unpleasant news or have to entice people to do things they'd prefer not to do. Over the years, I've had plenty of practice at being assertive and taken countless courses on people skills. Despite all the practice, I am repeatedly told in my performance reviews that I come across as too passionate and intimidating. This always seems bizarre to me. How could passion be considered negative? I've always considered my passion to be one of my strengths. I used to care about my work – surely that's what made me good at it? As for intimidating, I would never have considered myself to be intimidating in a work context. I am friendly and empathetic. Or completely deluded. The only time I could justifiably be accused of being intimidating was when I met my father's new girlfriend. But that was different – I was simply respecting the time-honoured tradition of grown-up daughters intimidating the poor woman their father has chosen as a substitute for their mother.

The last time a manager told me I was intimidating I asked him straight out if I intimidated him. He said, 'Of course not, but you do intimidate the other account directors.' I then asked all the other account directors if I intimidated them, and they each replied, 'Of course not, but you do intimidate the other account directors.'

I don't want to sound bitter, but it crossed my mind at the time that perhaps my feedback wouldn't have been so negative if I'd been a man – some men build their careers on being intimidating.

After that feedback, I started observing and admiring people who were calm in meetings. They seemed so in control, almost as if they were detached from the proceedings and viewing the situation from a distance. I tried to mimic them, but I struggled. It was hard to be calm and dispassionate when I cared so much about the outcome. But the up-side of my new 30-something attitude problem is that nobody can accuse me of being too passionate any more.

In one meeting recently, someone was being rude and hostile and accused my client and me of being so incompetent we couldn't arrange an orgy in a brothel let alone run the project. I let it all wash over me and systematically addressed all his concerns. At the end of it, my client asked me how I could remain so calm and composed. He looked at me as if I was Yoda. Not wanting to shatter his illusions, I didn't have the heart to tell him that I simply didn't care enough to mind. It's amazing how calm you can be when you don't give a shit.

Prior to this, when I'd admired my colleagues for being so calm I had attributed them with a greater level of maturity and wisdom than I had. I now wonder if I was being overly complimentary and that instead, like me, they'd just lost their give-a-shit too.

3

TROUBLESVILLE

'I want to have an affair,' Emma announces.

It all starts when she turns up on my doorstep late one night clutching a bottle of wine and an express ticket to Troublesville. While I have been distracting myself with the welfare of puppies, Emma has been compensating for her high-stress, soulless and unsatisfying working life by indulging in a world of vodka shooters and the temptation of fit bodies.

Emma's announcement is unexpected – not only because she has invested heavily in a five-year relationship and a mortgage with her boyfriend but also because she's always been so moralistic about infidelity. She has always considered cheating to be inexcusable.

'I'm a shit person,' she says. 'I can't believe I'm even considering this.'

Simon, the object of her infatuation, is high-energy, immature, irresponsible, inappropriate, crazy and the antithesis of her boyfriend. He is also a colleague. So not only is Emma considering breaking her no-cheating rule, she is also about to break her no-dating-in-the-workplace rule. Over-achiever that she is, Emma isn't content to break one rule when she can break two.

In the past, she has been so focused on her image and credibility in the workplace that she would never have considered shagging a colleague. Everyone knows that screwing the crew is the fastest way for a woman to sabotage her career. Linda Fiorentino memorably asserted in *The Last Seduction* that a woman loses 50 per cent of her authority in the workplace when her colleagues find out who she's sleeping with, and anecdotal evidence certainly suggests that she was right. Usually the man ends up a hero to his male workmates, while the woman ends up as the office joke. Maybe, however, Emma had lost her give-a-shit and was more interested in having a bit of fun than getting the corner office.

On this night, Emma and I grow up a little bit and realise that adult life is a lot more complicated than we had imagined in our moralising youth. It was easy to make rules about relationships and work behaviour when we were in our 20s. But now that we've hit our 30s, it has become a lot harder to abide by those rules. So I give Emma my full support, a box of condoms and insist she tells me every detail.

The next day, Emma breaks up with her boyfriend and begins her party-hard period – a blur of binge drinking, all-night parties and casual sex.

Simon lasts about two weeks – two glorious weeks filled with five-star-hotel romps and jewellery in aqua boxes. But after the initial excitement wears off, Emma realises it isn't going anywhere and doesn't really want it to anyway. So she moves on to the next one, and then the next one, and then the next one.

James lasts a couple of months because, according to Emma, he has 'the perfect male body'. I've only seen him with his clothes on, but even then I am inclined to agree. He is all brawn and no brains: exactly what Emma is looking for. I overhear him shagging Emma one night when they are sleeping in my spare bedroom – let me tell you, the boy has stamina. Emma's only regret with James is that she didn't take any photos of him naked.

I get a call from her one morning. She's just arrived home from a bar and finds a bus ticket in her pocket. Written on the ticket is 'Fabian – call me' and a phone number.

She'd been out the previous night with her latest man and had been approached by about a dozen men, so she can't quite remember which one was Fabian. This is an unusually high number of men hitting on her, even by Emma's standards. She puts it down to losing a massive amount of weight and fitting into her skinny jeans, the ones at the back of her wardrobe that haven't fitted properly for ten years but she's clung on to as a symbol of hope. As Emma is relaying the story to me, she notices that the bus ticket is a concession. 'This means he's either a student or a pensioner,' she says. 'Either way, this can't be good.'

But Emma isn't in the mood for being 'good', so she gives Fabian a call. In a sexy Latino accent, he tells her she is very beautiful and that he thinks they have a real connection. He invites her to his birthday party. Emma asks him how old he is going to be. He says 19. Emma is thrilled. Even though her life is completely chaotic and directionless, she still has what it takes to pull a teenager.

Emma doesn't go to Fabian's party. A 19 year old is too outrageous, even for her, but she keeps the bus ticket as a souvenir.

Weeks pass and Emma's 'phase' is turning into a lifestyle choice. Every time I see her, she is hungover or still drunk from the night before. She's lost an enormous amount of weight and looks pale, sickly and run-down. When I tell her how worried I am, she tells me to stop being so conservative. She admits that she feels tired and worn out but 'God, I'm having fun,' she says.

When I ask her why she is doing it, she says, 'Because I'm bored, Kase. I'm so bored.'

I can understand that. I'm bored too.

In *Man's Search for Meaning*, Viktor Frankl describes boredom as a symptom of an existential vacuum – a state of inner emptiness and meaninglessness. He also says it manifests itself in a pursuit of sexual pleasure . . . hmm . . .

Frankl was a Jewish psychologist who was interned in Auschwitz. Many of the insights in his book are based on his experiences during that time. If it were not for his intention to apply the learning from camp-life to ordinary life I would be ashamed to draw any comparison between his life and mine. While Emma and I have most certainly lost the sense of meaning in our lives, it seems absurd that our situation could be comparable to a concentration camp. But when I read Frankl's words about an existential vacuum, I can relate entirely.

Work fills up such a big part of our lives that when we don't care about it any more – when it has lost its meaning – we are left with a massive void. And patting ourselves on our backs and listing off all our achievements to date cannot possibly fill the void.

Frankl says that meaning is not created by having or achieving something but rather by striving towards and struggling for a worthwhile goal. It's the process of trying to accomplish something that creates meaning.

This is contrary to all the New Age self-help books that tell you to be present in your life and enjoy the now. When I look at my 'now', it's pretty damn good. Yet I don't have the inner peace and happiness the books say I should.

Looking back over our 20s, it's clear that Emma and I were happier when we were striving towards our 'worthwhile goal' – the career success that we have now. I suppose we had meaning in our lives because we were focusing our efforts on proving ourselves and climbing the corporate ladder. All through school, university and the early part of our careers, we were working towards this point. But now that we've reached the level of success at which we feel we've proved ourselves, we've stopped striving and therefore fallen into the vacuum of meaninglessness.

Frankl says that we all need to be striving and struggling for a worthwhile goal: a freely chosen task. So the most obvious thing to do is find a new worthwhile goal to strive for – something other than rescuing puppies in pet shops or dancing on bar stools. The only problem is that finding something meaningful to strive for is turning out to be a lot harder than we thought.

4

NOTHING TO DO BUT SHAG

A temporary reprieve from the day-to-day boredom and drudgery of my job comes when I am sent to another city to work on a new project. This involves catching the red-eye flight at 6 a.m. every Monday and returning on the 6 p.m. flight on Friday.

Unfortunately, my boredom with going to the same office every day, sitting at the same desk, staring at the same faded print on the wall, drinking from the same chipped mug is only replaced by the boredom of lonely hotel rooms and eating alone. Ahh . . . the glamour of business travel.

Before I started travelling for work, I thought that people who complained about business travel were such tossers. They flew all over the world, stayed in great hotels, ordered as much room service as they liked and watched porn movies that discreetly appeared on the bill as a service charge. Yet they felt the need to complain.

I have become one of those tossers.

Work travel has lost its excitement and glamour. When I worked in Europe, I was constantly travelling. The first 18 months were wonderful. I went to places I wouldn't normally go on my own, like Russia and the Baltics, and I met amazing people and saw amazing things. I relished talking to the locals and listening to their opinions on anything from marriage and politics to the etiquette of drinking vodka before midday.

I was in Poland on the tenth anniversary of when they kicked out the Russians, and I was fascinated by the views of the locals. I asked my colleague how life had changed since the fall of Communism. He said, 'Under Communism, everybody had enough money, but there was nothing to buy. Now there is everything to buy, but nobody has enough money. You tell me which is better.' I asked the woman spooning out sauerkraut in the staff restaurant for her impressions, and she said, 'Under Communism, we all had bread.' And the hotshot IT guy said, 'Thank fuck. I couldn't survive without broadband and American basketball.'

But after a while I felt like I'd been everywhere and seen everything. Now I find travelling for work tedious and boring, not to mention exhausting, inconvenient and lonely. And the truth is you very rarely get to see anything other than the airport, office and hotel room. Some consulting companies deliberately send their consultants to clients in another city because they work harder. When there is nothing to do in the evenings, there is no reason to leave the office, so people tend to stay there longer – either that or get shit-faced in the hotel bar and find someone to shag.

I've never shagged a colleague on a business trip, but I've certainly had plenty of opportunity. I used to find it flattering, now it just pisses me off. I hate it when a guy ruins a perfectly good working relationship or even a friendship simply because he's away from home and bored. Although, in fairness, there are plenty of women who are also desperate to find something (or someone) to do in the evenings.

I bump into a former client at a hotel bar. Susan is very clever, very professional and a little bit aloof. She is a blonde bombshell dressed in sensible shoes – the classic librarian archetype. I don't know anything about her personal life. We've only ever spoken about work matters, but when she offers to buy me a drink I jump at the chance of having somebody to talk to for the evening. One glass turns into one bottle, and then one more.

After a couple of serious drinks, Professional Susan shuffles in closer to me and puts her arm around me. She reaches down and starts rubbing her hands up and down my legs. I assume she is admiring my stockings, so I tell her which brand they are and show her the cute lace trim at the top. She slips her finger under the lace, and I realise she is more interested in the contents of my stockings. Her interest is confirmed when she starts fondling my breasts and kissing my neck. I try to disentangle our bodies without creating a scene. It feels like every pair of eyes in the bar is on us. Susan tries to stand up to order another bottle of wine, but she slips and knocks over all the glasses and bottles on the table. Wine and broken glass go everywhere. The barman points to the door, signalling for us to leave. I sense the disappointment of the other patrons as Susan and I stagger out of the bar.

Susan can barely stand up, and I doubt she will be able to get back to her hotel in that state. My only option is to escort her back to her hotel room. I hail a taxi – which Susan proceeds to vomit in, costing me 20 quid as a cleaning fee – and make our way to her hotel. As we walk through the lobby, Susan starts removing her clothes. I try to stop her, but I can't. I'm too busy holding her upright and picking up the clothes she is throwing on the ground. We reach Susan's room and she is naked on the top half. A group of business suits walk past us. They don't avert their eyes like gentlemen should.

As soon as we get into her hotel room, Susan strips off the remainder of her clothes and stands before me stark naked. Nothing. I feel nothing. I can't take my eyes off her, but all I can think about is how she has less cellulite than I have. Bitch.

My competitive thoughts are interrupted by the memory of my brother Michael telling me that I need to be whipped. Here is an opportunity for me to step outside my comfort zone and the constraints of my expectations and everybody else's. Susan doesn't have a whip in her hand, but surely a lesbian experience will provide the same opportunity for personal development. It will also make a really great story to tell my friends. Being bi is so cool right now.

But I can't. I just can't. As hot and cellulite-free as Susan is, I'm just not turned on. It also seems a bit opportunistic to experiment with a drunken woman in the hope that it will snap me out of my discontented funk. I realised that not only am I 30-something and over it, I am also as straight as an arrow.

I struggle against Susan's kisses and wandering hands as I put her into bed. Then I make my way to my hotel, alone and slightly disappointed about the opportunity I have wasted.

I see Susan the next day as I am boarding my flight home. I wave at her awkwardly and hurry onto the plane. As luck has it, it turns out she is seated next to me. What are the chances of that? I expect her to be embarrassed. I certainly am. But she doesn't seem fazed at all. She says she can't remember all the details from last night and casually enquires if anything happened between us. I say no, and she says that is a shame. She looks disappointed. Sometimes people really surprise me.

5

FAKING IT

Back in the office once more, despite my dismal attendance and attitude at work, by all accounts I am still doing a good job and impressing people.

My client satisfaction report states I have 'exceeded expectations', and I am commended for my leadership and knowledge of the subject matter. My client reports that he feels more confident and comfortable with the team's performance since I have joined. I also receive a big tick for team leadership – praised for empowering my team members and providing them with the opportunity to grow. I used to be crappy at delegation, always craving and fighting for extra responsibility and wanting to do everything myself. Now I am happy to stand back and let my team carry the load. Being praised for it is unexpected. Who knew that losing my give-a-shit would make me a master of delegation?

My glowing report card has the opposite effect from what you might expect – I am more demotivated and resentful than ever.

I like to think that I'm pretty good at my job and have enough ability and experience to hold my own in almost any situation, but to be praised and rewarded for doing virtually nothing except showing up to meetings highlights the ludicrousness of my work. My client report and the performance review that follows is a complete farce. I lose respect for the individuals involved and the whole performance management process because I can so easily manipulate them.

This sounds childish, but I want people to expect more from me. I want to be required to switch my brain on at work, and I don't want to so easily get away with faking it. I used to work my arse off at work, now I hardly do anything at all. Yet nobody seems to notice the difference, much less care about it. I should be amused by the absurdity, but I'm not. I'm struck by a whole new level of meaninglessness.

Emma is faking it, too. The penny has dropped that she is good enough at her job to get away with doing half as much work as she used to do. At a very young age, Emma learned that even though people ask for 'all', it's often good enough to give them 'half'. When her mother said she had to eat all her vegetables before she could have dessert, her mother was always satisfied when she'd eaten half. It is only now that Emma realises she can apply her strategy for not eating vegetables to her job.

Because Emma is in charge of a part of the business that other people don't know much about, she is able to make up excuses for not delivering her work on time. She blames delays on legal issues and problems with suppliers, and because her colleagues don't know any better they give her the benefit of the doubt.

Sometimes it isn't a matter of being late; she just doesn't do things at all. Everybody on the leadership team has to present a business plan for the year ahead. Emma makes up a cock-and-bull story about how the structure of the business plan doesn't fit her line of business so she can't prepare a business plan. Instead of telling her to modify the template, her colleagues give her credit for being innovative and having an in-depth knowledge of her business.

At the beginning of the year she was supposed to submit the criteria on which she'll be judged for her bonus. She didn't get around to submitting the criteria, so now, when her bonus is due to be paid, she writes the criteria retrospectively to include the few things that she has achieved. When Emma tells me she's received her full bonus, she justifies herself by saying, 'The system allowed me to manipulate it, so I did.' Before adding, 'Do you think that makes me a sociopath?'

I honestly believe that most of the people I have ever worked with have been faking it. People don't just fake the amount of time and effort they put into something, they also fake their skills and abilities. In my younger days, I naively made the assumption that my managers and the leaders of organisations were competent. I assumed that they had risen up the ranks due to merit. Even when some of their decisions and behaviour seemed foolish or ill advised, I would give them the benefit of the doubt, believing that I lacked the experience and insight to understand. Over the last couple of years, however, I've seen so many examples of what I first thought to be beyond my understanding turn out to be nothing more than incompetence. I can't tell you how disappointing and deflating it is to realise that the people leading me don't know any more about what they are doing than I do. In some cases, they know even less. I realise that it might sound pretty cynical and unfair to have such a low opinion of my colleagues, but I can think of numerous examples that justify my attitude.

For example, I once had a manager who asked me to think more slowly. He said that when he had been stewing over a problem for days and I walked into the room and gave him an answer in a matter of minutes it made him feel bad. So he asked me to stop it. He was a lovely man who seemed to me to have reached his position of leadership by just refusing to vacate his chair for 20 years. Everyone around him either left, retired or died.

When I first started consulting, an account director pulled me aside and told me the secret to success. He said, 'Babe, in this business you have to fake it until you make it.' This was good advice, especially when I was once given an assignment to perform the role of an accountant, scrutinising investment proposals worth millions of pounds. Not only had I never studied accounting, I had only studied dummies' maths at school. The extent of my mathematical ability was working out percentage discounts in the Christmas sales. In fact, when I was recruited into the consulting company I failed the maths component of the entrance exam. It was terribly embarrassing when the human resource manager phoned me and said, 'I haven't done this before, but let's just say I've *lost* your maths test.' Because I had aced the language and problem-solving component of the test he decided to give me another shot at the maths part. He also said, 'Do you think, maybe, you could study for it this time?'

I explained to my account director, who was trying to convince me that it was OK to masquerade as an accountant, that I was allergic to numbers, but he said that nobody else was available and he would really appreciate me 'going outside my comfort zone'. This was code for 'if you do it I'll make sure you get a good bonus', so I spent the weekend reading *Accounting for Dummies* and showed up at my client's office on Monday and introduced myself to everyone as the new accountant. Nobody thought to question this, so I sat down at my desk, sharpened my pencil and went to work. I enjoyed this role-playing exercise for the first month because I was on such a steep learning curve and was fully engaged trying to disguise my incompetence. I certainly didn't exceed expectations, but I did well enough to get by (although it'll be years before the fallout from any bad investments are realised, so it's impossible to say this with absolute certainty), and after a while it became routine and just like any other job: dull.

It is clear to me that I am happier at work when I'm being challenged and stretched. I was happier when I was still striving to prove myself and achieve all the things I thought I always wanted. I get more pleasure and satisfaction in striving to achieve than having achieved. But I have stopped learning and striving at work – most of the time I can leave my brain at home and nobody will even notice. Sure, each client I work for is slightly different or has unique problems, but after the first couple of weeks on a project it always becomes routine.

Maybe this is the answer to my 30-something-and-over-it crisis. Maybe I just need to find a more challenging job. I decide to apply for a job at a strategy consulting company. These organisations are the 'thinkers' rather than the 'doers' of the consulting world. If you've ever been through a restructure, these guys are the ones that came up with the plan and then left somebody else to deal with the mess of implementing it. They pride themselves on their innovative thinking and problem solving. They also pride themselves on working their consultants to the bone. I think that perhaps I can tolerate the ridiculously long hours if I am compensated by being challenged.

Strategy consulting companies are notoriously difficult to get into. Everyone I know who's worked for them has had a brain the size of a planet (and they're all a little bit eccentric, now that I think about it). To prepare, I buy a book on how to 'ace the case' interview. Case interviews are where they give you a real-world problem and you have to solve it on the spot. The cases vary from working out how many golf balls fit in a Boeing 747 (I'm serious) to improving the profits of a multinational. I work really hard at my preparation. I stumble through about 20 practice case exercises and relearn how to multiply fractions and calculate velocity and probability.

Two intelligent and impressive women conduct my interview. They do a good job selling the organisation to me, saying all the magic phrases like 'problem solving', 'intellectually challenging' and 'personal growth'. It seems like the type of place that will really challenge me, and I am excited by the prospect. There is only one part of the interview that I find slightly alarming. One of the interviewers tells me how the company values work/life balance, and to illustrate the point she tells me about their mobile workforce – meaning that people often leave the office in time to have dinner with their partners and children, and then they can continue working from home in the evening instead of staying at the office. Whoo hoo.

I am given two case interviews, and at the end of them I am told that I have come to the same conclusions as the consultants had when they were working for the clients. I leave the interview feeling like I have 'aced the case'. I am expecting to be asked back for the second round. I am to be disappointed.

After an agonising week of waiting for the phone to ring, Karen, one of the interviewers, phones me to give me the bad news. She tells me that I clearly have excellent business acumen and judgement, and am certainly the type of person they recruit; however, I didn't do very well on the case interviews. My thinking was not methodical or sequential enough. She tries to soften the blow by telling me that doing case interviews is a skill, and I simply need more practice at them. I don't mention the 20 I had practised in the lead-up to the interview. Since Karen said that I am capable of passing the case interview if I have more practice, I ask her if I can re-interview after I work on my case-interview technique some more. She says no, so I assume I'm not as capable as she had first claimed.

I feel pretty deflated, partly because of the rejection but more by the fact that I'm not any closer to figuring out what I should do with my life. Working for this company would have enabled me to determine whether or not learning and intellectual challenge are the keys to my happiness at work. I stew over my missed opportunity for a couple of weeks and then decide that I should just ring Karen and ask her if this sort of work fulfils her.

Karen is 32 and had joined the organisation as a graduate, rocketing through the ranks. It is clear that this is not just a job to her; it is a way of life. 'I have a huge commitment to [the company],' she says. 'I'm loyal to it because I started my career here and they've looked after me.' She says that the organisation 'puts its tentacles' into every aspect of her life. I think this is an interesting choice of words. She says she has formed deep bonds with her colleagues due to the high-pressure environment and long hours they work.

I ask if she feels like she is wasting the best years of her life because of the long hours, and without missing a beat she says, 'No. Because what else would I be doing?'

Last year, Karen had some moments of uncertainty where she questioned her career and began to think about having a family. 'I was a bit bored in my job at the time and I was just looking for a reason to leave, so I started thinking about kids.' But a colleague pulled her aside and convinced her that wanting to leave the workforce was not a very good reason to have kids. Karen is relieved that she 'escaped motherhood' because she is now enjoying her job again.

'Opting out seemed like a good idea at the time, but there is so much else to experience and my job allows me to do that,' Karen says. Even though she plans to have kids in the future, she considers motherhood to be a compromise. 'Having kids will take me out of the workforce. I don't want to be one of those women who never comes back.

'If you opt out, who are you going to be? A mother? What else?' she says. 'I've always been this career person who does interesting things and meets interesting people. I can't imagine not being that person.'

I am shocked and slightly outraged at Karen's low opinion of motherhood, which makes me realise how much I've changed in the last few months. I am ashamed to admit this, but 12 months ago I would have agreed with Karen's view on motherhood – a cop-out from the workforce, the loss of identity and a betrayal of the sisterhood. What was the point of being given all these wonderful opportunities in life if you're going to waste them by 'just' being a mother? I used to think a pram was a symbol of no ambition, no status and a bleak future.

I don't know whether my biological clock is starting to tick more loudly or losing my give-a-shit at work has made me think more broadly, but now I view motherhood as a noble and honourable profession. I'm not sure I'm ready for it right now, but I can't think of anything that could be more important and more meaningful than raising and socialising the next generation.

I have friends who are planning families and are terrified at the thought of not earning an income for a while. Partly they don't want to be dependent on their partners but they also worry about not 'contributing' in the relationship. It seems their definition of 'contribution' is limited to a financial one. They don't seem to consider the time, love and patience that they devote to raising a child to be a contribution to the relationship. We've bought into the idea that activities that do not earn money are worthless, and it seems to me we need a new measuring stick.

Oliver James in *Affluenza* suggests that the devaluation of the status of mothering and our belief that only paid work is a source of self-esteem is the key reason why women are twice as likely to be depressed than men. It's tragic to think that we place more value on our contribution to the economy than we do on our contribution to society. How did we become so fucked up?

Karen has considered making a social contribution from a work perspective. 'Occasionally, when tragic events happen in the world I think, "What am I doing about it – nothing." But then time passes and I get involved in my own life again.'

Her sister works for a pro-choice organisation, so Karen feels like she has enough well-meaning people around her who fill the meaning void. She's also seen first hand that working on something meaningful doesn't necessarily make you happy. 'I've seen the frustration my sister goes through dealing with the bureaucracy and trying to get things done. I also know that she'd like to work in the corporate sector so she can earn more money.'

Unlike me, Karen still has career boxes to tick: she still has career goals she needs to achieve. She is working towards making partner. In the consulting world, partners are the people who call the shots and own the yachts. 'It's a huge challenge,' she says. 'I love being challenged.' She qualifies her pursuit of partnership by saying that she doesn't need to make partner to prove herself. Instead, she needs the challenge that is required to do it.

I used to feel the same way Karen did about work. I distinctly remember saying in my early 20s that I didn't want a job; I wanted a career. I was searching for that all-consuming workplace that would define me, give me status and connect me to like-minded people. And the few times in my career where I've found that have been very happy times.

I ask Karen if she is happy and without hesitation she says, 'Yes, I am.'

I genuinely envy her enthusiasm and passion for work. It is obvious that she is a lot more fulfilled than I am. But when I listen to her I can hear my old self talking. The Kasey of 12 months ago would have been just as driven to achieve corporate success and dismissive of the value of motherhood. A year ago, I too would have linked my identity and self-worth to my career performance and income.

I hate to admit this, partly because I genuinely like Karen and partly because I don't want to sound bitter about being rejected by her organisation, but I walk away from our conversation with a sense of superiority. I feel superior because I now have the insight and courage to question my work and its value in my life; I am no longer content to blindly follow the path that was prescribed for me. I wonder if Karen would be quite so happy if she had a little more self-awareness and really thought about what she is doing and why.

I am always in two minds about self-awareness. On one hand, I think it's overrated – I certainly was a lot happier when I wasn't so reflective – but at the same time, to avoid thinking about things because they are challenging and painful seems like we are limiting our potential. I also view self-insight as a bit like an insurance policy: something to prevent me getting to 80 and looking back over my life with a sense of regret. Regret is surely the loneliest emotion in the world, because you have nobody to blame but yourself.

As I say goodbye to Karen, the nasty, competitive bitch inside me overpowers my mind, and I think, 'For someone so smart, she's not doing a lot of thinking.'

6

WHAT'S YOUR BABY?

I arrange to have lunch with Godfrey in the hope that he'll have some words of wisdom for me. Godfrey is only a few years older than I am, but he always seems so wise – as if he has the benefit of a couple of lifetimes of experience.

He is also a gentleman, as if he has risen from the pages of a Jane Austen novel. If ever you were to lose faith in men, Godfrey is the one to restore it. I melted when he once told me about his first meeting with his wife. 'No offence,' he said, 'but when she walked into the room I thought that she was the most beautiful woman I'd ever seen.' How could I take offence at that?

I got to know Godfrey really well a couple of years ago – or perhaps I should say he got to know me really well – on a business trip when I'd had a few too many gins. He asked me how I was, and I, well, told him.

My eyes welled up with tears, and I started to shake. Godfrey sat there patiently listening to me pour out my heart about how my father had recently walked out on my mother and now had a new life that didn't seem to have room for me in it; how my boyfriend had just moved to the Amazon rainforest with no plans to return; and how my mother had just tried to hang herself with a telephone cord in the flat I'd bought a few weeks earlier.

In hindsight, this was probably a little too much information to give a colleague. When he asked me how I was, I should have just replied 'Fine, thanks.'

Godfrey was a champion. He put his arm around me in a big-brotherly sort of way and told me that I'd be OK. He suggested I see a psychologist but warned me that it would be the most confronting and difficult experience of my life. He assured me it would be worth it, because one day the sun would come out and it would shine brighter than I ever knew it could. He was right on both counts.

Therapy was hell. I've lost count of how many days I sobbed uncontrollably on the couch and how many nights I dulled the pain with a dinner of gin and ice cream in the bathtub. But just as Godfrey had predicted, one day the grey clouds parted, and I stepped out into the sunshine. I wasn't the same person after that. I felt like I was new and improved and I could handle anything – even being 30-something and over it.

I am hoping Godfrey will provide me with the same sort of profound and life-changing advice as last time.

'You need a baby,' he says.

I look at him in disbelief. I have vivid memories of him declaring that neither he nor his wife wanted kids, and even though my views on motherhood have changed I'm not sure I want to be one. And I don't want to believe that the answer to my 30-something crisis is as simple as getting knocked up.

'It doesn't have to be a real one,' he clarifies. 'It can also be a metaphorical baby.'

He says I need to find something to grow and invest in for the next 20 years – something to spend my money on and my time thinking about. I need something to devote myself to, to give me meaning. There is that word again!

'But I don't know what will give me meaning,' I say.

'I do. It's obvious,' he says. 'It's writing. I've seen the way your face lights up when you talk about writing. You love it; it's your passion.'

I do love writing. I have story ideas and unfinished manuscripts stashed away in storage boxes and on hard drives. I once wrote a complete novel in airports and planes when I was travelling for work. I was going to be a writer when I grew up – that was if the whole Wonder Woman or fairy thing didn't work out. At one point, I was certain I'd end up as the speechwriter for the Secretary General of the United Nations. I even sent a letter to Bono asking him to partner me to my high-school dance because I wanted to talk to him about his song lyrics. He said no. I know: I couldn't believe he turned me down either.

My first job was in public relations, where I wrote articles for a trade publication and various other bits and pieces. I loved it. I got such a buzz seeing my work in print. But I lasted in public relations for about two minutes before I sniffed out opportunities to work on IT projects. At the time, I told myself I was looking for new challenges, but if I'm really honest I must admit it wasn't the challenge that turned me on, it was the money. I equated success with money and leapfrogged from job to job with bigger and bigger pay cheques.

I've since read enough self-help books to know that money does not equate to happiness. Susan Maushart in her excellent book *What Women Want Next* says that the link between income and happiness is almost laughably weak. She refers to a study to determine if those with yuppie lifestyles were happier. The study found that those who rated a high income, occupational success and prestige over having close friends and a good marriage were twice as likely to describe themselves as unhappy.

When I look at Chris's lifestyle, I am filled with both envy and pride. I love reading his writing – it's so clever and articulate, which really turns me on. Good writing is like porn to me. But while it's really sexy when *he* does it, the idea of *me* writing for a living is terrifying. I've invested the last ten years following a different path, and, even though I'm not thrilled with the destination, I'm not sure I want to go back to first base and start all over again. And I'm pretty sure I couldn't afford to live on first base either.

I know all the books about downsizing, sea-changing or living your dream claim that this lifestyle choice doesn't have to equate to poverty. Apparently it is possible to do what you love and get paid for it. I like to think of myself as a pretty resourceful person, but I can't imagine finding anything else to do – whether I love it or not – that will pay me as much as I am earning now. Even if I start my own business, build an empire and become totally loaded, it will still take years before the cash starts rolling in. Despite what all the books and Emma and Michael are saying, the realist in me knows that any change in profession will seriously reduce my income.

And right now I need every penny. I'm broke.

7

THE BRINK OF BANKRUPTCY

My financial situation is a disgrace. If I lost my job, I'd be bankrupt within six weeks.

In my second year in the workforce, I was earning as much as my mother, who is a schoolteacher. In my fourth year, I was earning more than my parents combined. My dad is a teacher-in-charge of a school. People raise whole families on what I get as a bonus payment, yet I spend every penny I earn, and some. I have massive credit-card debt and zero savings.

How can this be? How on earth did I become so financially irresponsible?

What I consider to be normal and reasonable has shifted over time. In my early years of working, it would have to be a very special occasion for me to eat out, and even then I'd order the cheapest thing on the menu and only drink water. I used to hate it when we'd split the bill, because I'd end up paying for somebody else's wine.

Now I eat out all the time. It isn't unusual for me to eat out all three meals in a day. And somewhere along the way I've stopped looking at the prices on the menu, too. I just order whatever I want and, instead of drinking water, I drink cocktails. Each year, Emma and I go on a tropical holiday together and make it our mission to drink every cocktail on the menu. It hadn't occurred to me before now that this is extravagant.

In the past, the idea of catching a taxi wouldn't have even crossed my mind. I used public transport all the time, and if I missed the last train home I'd walk. Now, I drive and pay for parking, or if I have to wait more than ten minutes for a bus I'll catch a cab. I tell myself that my time is more valuable than the taxi fare. Once upon a time I even bought standing tickets at the opera or snuck in at half time for free; now, it's the best seats in the stalls every time. I've fallen into the trap of spending money I don't have, on things I don't need, to plug a void it can never fill.

In her book *I Could Do Anything, If I Only Knew What It Was*, Barbara Sher refers to people like me as 'Fast Trackers' – high-earning, high-status professionals who look successful on the outside but are miserable inside. Fast Trackers like me are also financially irresponsible. We buy beautiful things such as cars, clothes, houses, soft furnishings and holidays as consolation prizes for our unfulfilled lives – toys to try to compensate for the huge part of our lives that we've sacrificed for our professional success. It is somewhat comforting to know it isn't just me who lives like this.

My greatest extravagance is books. I can't walk past a bookshop without going in and buying a couple. I have more books than I have time to read; and my shoe collection isn't half bad either. I have become one of those vacuous, materialist yuppies I used to despise when I was at university. But I am in good company – my friends are just the same. I recently went shopping with a friend who bought four pairs of shoes and a handbag on impulse, which came to a grand total of £2,000. I swear the entire transaction took less than 15 minutes. Sure, they were handcrafted from the finest leather, but that was £133 per minute. Not bad. At the time, it didn't even occur to me that it was dysfunctional.

Po Bronson in his book *What Should I Do With My Life?* interviewed a bunch of people who were suffering through highly paid jobs they hated in order to save money so they could quit and then pursue their dream. Bronson said that he couldn't find any evidence of these plans ever eventuating. It seemed that people never reached the point where they considered themselves to be wealthy enough to chuck it all in. And their dream was only ever just that – a dream.

I've seen an extreme case of what Bronson is talking about in one of my friend's boyfriends. A few years ago, Jessica met a billionaire on a plane. It was an unusual situation in that she had been upgraded to business class (she only ever travelled economy) and he couldn't get a first-class seat, so he had to slum it in business. She didn't know who he was when they first started dating. Several weeks later when she agreed to visit him in Asia, she realised he wasn't your average guy. It was the private jet he sent to collect her that tipped her off. It turned out he was a multi-billionaire with high stakes in the media and energy industries.

Their romance progressed in the usual way with breakfasts in London, lunches on the private jet and dinners in New York. After a few months, she moved to Asia to live with him. It wasn't the fairytale she had expected.

Jessica could accept the long hours he worked and the limited time they spent together, but when he missed her father's funeral and couldn't make it to Christmas because he was too busy doing deals, things started to unravel. He assured her that his crazy working hours were only temporary and that when he had earned enough money he would retire and they could live the good life together. She asked him how much money was 'enough'. When he couldn't answer, she left.

Bronson observed that the people who made dramatic career shifts to follow their passion just did it, regardless of whether or not they could afford it. This is how my brother Michael lives his life, too. If you tried to plan Michael's life on a piece of paper or his earnings on a balance sheet, you'd never do it. Yet he's been doing it all his life. He's like the bumblebee – he flies anyway.

Even though I know that if I wait until I am completely secure before making a change I'll probably never do it, I am sure that following my dreams – whatever they may be – will be a lot more pleasant if I'm not broke. I need to get my finances in order.

The first thing I do is work out a budget. I've never had a personal budget before. I've managed multi-million-dollar budgets for projects at work, but it has never occurred to me to manage one for myself.

Writing down everything I spend in a month does wonders to highlight my extravagances and 'quick wins' on my balance sheet. I change my health insurance policy, broadband plan and phone plan over to cheaper options. I stop taking taxis and start eating at home more often, and feed my book addiction from the library. It turns out I have a library just two blocks from my house. It's amazing what you don't see when you're not looking.

Discovering the library simply because my perspective has changed is symbolic of my thrisis. I wonder what else I can discover about myself and the world around me now that I am losing the tunnel vision that has prevented me from looking anywhere except up the corporate ladder.

Autumn

'Everyone must take time to sit and watch the leaves turn'
– Elizabeth Lawrence

8

COMPULSORY FUN

As the autumn leaves start to turn, frustration and self-loathing set in. How is it that the trees can evolve into a new state and yet I cannot? Other than a failed job interview and a pathetic lesbian experience, nothing has changed for me. I'm still stuck in my void of meaninglessness and resentment, and even though the weeks and months are flying by, every day feels like an eternity. I step up my search for my give-a-shit and resolve to make more time to think about, talk about and read about why I'd lost it in the first place.

My first opportunity for investigation arises when one of my clients requests that I join him in observing the inner workings of his company's call centre. He is about to implement changes that will affect the staff in the call centre and wants to assess how disruptive the changes will be. I jump at the chance to go with him – not only to look for my own answers but also because I feel like I am embarking on an anthropological study. I am intrigued to see what a call centre is like from the other side of the phone line.

I have pretty fixed views about call centres – modern-day sweatshops, dens of misery for the working class. I expect to find it full of miserable, broken and hopeless people. I find the opposite; well, on the surface anyway.

Walking into the call centre is like visiting a kindergarten. Brightly coloured pictures and montages line the walls, and streamers and balloons hang from the ceiling. I am paired up with John, which means I am given my own headset so I can listen in on his calls while I view his computer screen over his shoulder. John looks to be in his late teens or early 20s. He hasn't grown out of his acne yet and is decked out in a polyester suit and a cartoon-character tie. I hope there aren't any exposed flames in the kitchen. He shakes my hand, flashes a big grin full of braces and clicks the button to initiate his next call. He only has time to chat to me while he is waiting for his next victim . . . I mean valued customer . . . to answer. His inactivity is being timed, and he can't afford to waste valuable minutes talking to me. He is on track to get his bonus this month, and a high inactivity rating will jeopardise his chances.

I ask about his bonus, and he flicks over to a complex spreadsheet of numbers and formulae. If all goes well, he is on track to get £50 this month.

John can choose which phone list he works. Customers are split according to demographics, and the secret to John's success is that he always works the 'old fogies' list. Apparently they're much easier to sell to. When Mr Wilson answers John's call, I discover why.

From reading John's screen I can see that Mr Wilson is 89 years old and on a pension. I listen to the conversation:

JOHN: Good morning, this is John from X Company. Is that Mr Wilson?

MR WILSON: No. Mr Wilson isn't home.

JOHN: That's a shame, because I'm ringing to see if I can save Mr Wilson some money on his phone bill.

MR WILSON: How much money?

JOHN: Unfortunately, I'm not authorised to discuss it with you. I can only speak to Mr Wilson about it. Do you know when he'll be home?

MR WILSON: You can talk to me about Mr Wilson's affairs.

JOHN: I wish I could, but I'm only authorised to discuss it with Mr Wilson. Do you know when he'll be home?

MR WILSON: OK, you've got me. I'm Mr Wilson.

John doesn't seem at all surprised by Mr Wilson's behaviour and asks some security questions to validate his identity. He toggles to a new screen on his computer and brings up Mr Wilson's phone records.

JOHN: I can see here, Mr Wilson, that you make a lot of calls from your mobile phone to 0845 numbers.

MR WILSON: That's right, I like to bet on the horses. I need to phone in to find out how my gee-gees are doing.

JOHN: Is there a reason you use your mobile phone and not your home phone?

MR WILSON: I like to call when I'm in the garden.

By the end of the call John has sold Mr Wilson a two-year broadband contract (so he can track the racing results online), and it is wireless of course, so he can do it from the garden. It is unclear if Mr Wilson knows what the Internet is or even owns a computer.

John hangs up the phone and punches the air, crying out 'YES!' His teammates gather around and pat him on the back. 'This is why I love my job,' John says to me. 'I really get to help people.'

Despite the obvious morality issues, I have to admire John's sales skills. I listen to him close deal after deal and know there is no way I could have made those sales, even if I'd wanted to.

John tells me that he is soon to be promoted to a new team in the call centre. At the moment, he is in the highest-performing centre in the company, but soon he will move to the highest-performing team.

'I'm going to be in the best of the best,' John says. 'I can't wait.'

I am amazed by the up-beat, high-energy atmosphere in the call centre, and totally freaked out by it as well. The place looks like something Aldous Huxley conjured into existence.

I can't get my head around how these people, who have timed toilet breaks and who rip off old and vulnerable people for a living, can be so happy about their jobs. I get a clue when I read the poster on the back of the toilet door. It is titled 'Well-being News' and states that 'scientists have proved that smiling makes you feel happier, even when you're feeling down'.

Another insight into the call-centre culture comes when I see the horrible book called *The Secret* taking pride of place on the team leader's desk. *The Secret* is about the Law of Attraction, which is essentially being able to manifest whatever you want simply by thinking positively. It seems to me that this universal law is about as believable as the economic law of puppies that the woman in the pet shop told me about. Other than making self-help gurus obscenely rich, the Law of Attraction is based on the premise that the universe will give you whatever you ask for. Through your thoughts, you can tap into the universe's gift catalogue and order whatever you like – a new car, a satisfying job, a loving partner and even naturally correcting eyesight.

As much as I rubbish the idea, there is something quite appealing and enticing about this concept. I must confess that I hold out a glimmer of hope each morning that there will be a new car in my driveway with a map inside that will direct me to my dream job. The notion that there is indeed such an easy answer to what is proving to be a complex problem is incredibly seductive.

When *The Secret* was first released, Chris reviewed it for a newspaper. We decided to test the Law of Attraction. As advised in the book, we made our requests tangible and measurable, so I asked the universe for an iPod and Chris asked the universe for an extra two inches. In case you're wondering, neither of them materialised.

As far as I am concerned, the most appalling part of *The Secret* is the victim blaming. Things that go wrong in your life are entirely your fault because you manifested it yourself – if you had more positive thoughts, it wouldn't have happened to you in the first place. You know Viktor Frankl and all his mates in Auschwitz? Well, it seems to me that if you take *The Secret* to its logical conclusion, it was their fault they were interned, because if their thoughts had been more positive they could have been sipping piña coladas in the South Pacific instead. Or if you are involved in a car accident: bingo, it was those pesky negative thoughts you have been having.

John tells me that people who are negative or cynical don't last long in his team – they only work with 'can do' people because 'fun is compulsory in this call centre'. Maybe they are afraid of a negative person manifesting something terrible like ethics or authenticity or, heaven forbid, an extra couple of minutes for toilet breaks.

The visit to the call centre knocks me off balance. By my estimation, these people are doing one of the worst jobs in the developed world and loving it. I've read articles about the massive turnover rates in call centres and the equally high rates of depression and obesity for those poor sods who can't or won't leave. But from what I can tell, John and his mates are a hell of a lot happier than I am. It doesn't seem to matter to them that they have crap pay, crap conditions, crap career paths and are treated like children.

I can see the appeal of working in a non-hierarchical environment with your peer group. Presumably it would be like hanging out with friends – literally patting one another on the back every time you do 'good work'. But I am pretty sure that a pat on the back and toilet-door wisdom are not enough to fulfil me. The thought of showing up there every day for eight hours of compulsory fun is enough to drive me to snorting the toner in the photocopier cartridges.

In the same way that Karen from the strategy consulting company perplexes me, I can't understand their happiness and fulfilment in their jobs. But I envy it. If happiness is the ultimate goal, then they are a lot closer to Nirvana than I am.

9

GREAT EXPECTATIONS

'Maybe you just expect too much from work,' Rodney says earnestly as he begins to draw concentric circles with his finger on the table to illustrate his point. Typical bloody consultant – has a diagram for everything.

Rodney is happy in his job. I can't understand this because we are a similar age and do similar work, yet he appears to be untarnished by this 30-something jaded discontent.

'Happiness and meaning come from four things that you need to keep in balance – family and friends, work, hobbies and your health,' Rodney says. 'I get meaning from my relationships with my wife and family, I volunteer for Oxfam and I play a lot of sport. I enjoy my job, but I don't expect it to be the only thing in my life that fulfils me.'

Initially I think Rodney is deluded. Surely the solution to finding happiness in the workplace is not as simple as drawing a diagram and lowering your expectations. When we spend so much of our lives at work, and we study so hard preparing for the job in the first place, to be content with anything less than total fulfilment seems like an exercise in self-delusion, or a sell-out.

Rodney isn't the only one advocating the lowering of expectations as an antidote for employment misery. Nigel Marsh is also a believer. Marsh is a former CEO of an advertising agency. He was retrenched and claims that by losing his job he found his life – and he has written two revealing and entertaining books about his experience: *Fat, Forty and Fired* and *Observations of a Very Short Man*. His advice is that if you want to make lasting changes in your life, you should start by lowering your standards.

I ask Rodney where he sees himself in five years' time, and to my amazement he responds with: 'I see myself with a couple of kids, owning my own home, still learning new things and achieving at work, and I'll still be involved with Oxfam and my sports clubs.' In all the times I've asked this question, he is the first person to describe his whole life rather than defaulting to his career. Maybe Rodney's four-circle approach is working for him.

We can't all be as lucky as Rodney in having great families and good health. But maybe he is onto something with the hobbies. I've always thought that there should be a proportional relationship between satisfaction and time. Surely I should expect more satisfaction from work than I do from my hobbies, because I spend more time at work? Rodney and I have opposing views on satisfaction – I am like an accountant measuring satisfaction based on units of time, while Rodney is the aesthete focusing on quality rather than quantity.

I decide to try Rodney's approach for myself and attempt to focus more attention on my hobbies. There is one small problem: I don't have any. Where have all my hobbies gone? I used to do ballet, amateur theatre, debating and student politics. I haven't done any of these things since I started working. There has been no time for frivolous things like a hobby; I had a career to build. What a loser I have become.

Realising that I haven't had any hobbies for over ten years, I decide to rectify the situation immediately. According to Barbara Sher in *I Could Do Anything If I Only Knew What It Was*, taking up new hobbies is a good way to meet new people and try new things that could also help you figure out what to do with your life. This makes sense. How am I supposed to find out what else I should do in the world if I don't know anybody who does anything different?

I realise how small my world has become after a conversation with a manager at work. He tells me that he's never met an unemployed person. I chuckle smugly at his limited social sphere until I think about my own. I only know people who do what I do. All the people I mix with are tertiary educated, middle class and mostly perform some kind of information-shuffling work in the private sector. We have the same political outlook, drink the same wine, read the same books, laugh at the same corporate wanker jokes – some of us even have the same breed of dog.

With the dual purpose of getting a hobby and peering over the back fence of my life, I join a beginners' tap-dancing class. It is run by an ex-showgirl now in her 60s. She is outrageous and eccentric – in a good way – and has legs to kill for. She promises that tapping will get rid of cellulite. I buy a pair of bright red tap shoes, and I look hot!

I am the odd one out in the tap class, being the only one who works in an office. Some of the women are nurses but mostly they are 50-something, married, kids-off-our-hands, tennis-on-Tuesdays, well-bred elites. They are lovely ladies who smell of pressed linen and take a lot of pride in their rose gardens.

Tap classes are a blast. I learn how to do time steps, that tapping does not get rid of cellulite and where to get discount botox injections, but I'm not any closer to working out what I want to do with my life. And I certainly am not any happier about showing up to work every day.

Perhaps I chose the wrong hobby? I keep stumbling across people who find meaning and fulfilment in either playing or coaching sport. But while I love the idea of being sporty, I've never been able to handle a ball without somebody questioning the quality of my gene pool.

In contrast, my friend Kelly (possibly the most well-rounded, happy person I know) coaches and manages a girls' football team. Kelly is a couple of years older than I am and is without doubt the most efficient person I've ever worked with. She is one of those annoying people who manages to read all her emails, action them and file them on the same day they are sent. We worked together on a project a few years ago. She was marketing communications manager at the time and could churn out newsletters and press releases at lightning speed.

I'd lost touch with Kelly until I notice her name in the email directory at my client organisation. I send her an email to say hello and to find out what she is doing these days. She replies in less than five minutes. Some things never change.

Kelly is still working in marketing communications, and she is still actively involved with the football club. In her email, she writes that she loves her job. Loves! She uses the words 'loves' and 'job' in the same sentence and she's in her 30s. I call her immediately and arrange a time to have lunch.

'I came out of university thinking that I'd change the world,' Kelly says. 'I assumed I was going to do that through my work, but then I realised that I am already making a difference – I'm doing it through the football club.'

Kelly seems to attract wayward kids into her football club in the way that some women attract stray cats. She spends a lot of time training them up to kick balls without being laughed at and helping them to feel included and valued. 'I've really made a difference with some of these kids,' she says. 'Some of them were on the wrong track, and I turned them around. And now I watch them befriend and support the new kids with the skills and confidence I taught them. That's satisfying.'

It took Kelly a while to realise that she wasn't ambitious. She kidded herself for a while, trying to climb the ladder, and ended up in management with a team of people. 'I don't like managing people,' she says. 'There's no way I want my boss's job.' Her boss is 35, female and brilliant, and Kelly clearly has a lot of respect for her, but her boss spends her life in the office and that's not the life Kelly wants. 'I want a job that will fund my lifestyle but not interfere with it,' she says.

From the outside looking in, Kelly's life is full and rich. As well as her football club she has an extensive network of friends that she speaks of fondly, and three godchildren. She also does courses at the local community college. So far she's done courses in knitting, shiatsu massage and picture framing.

Kelly says that even if she were totally loaded with cash she'd still work. She enjoys mixing with different types of people at work that she wouldn't normally meet in her social circle. She also needs the intellectual challenge of working. 'At work, I'm constantly achieving something,' she says. 'I feel like I'm making a difference. Sure, it's not like saving somebody's life, but I love communicating, and what I communicate meets the needs of people.'

She particularly enjoys her current job because her boss gives her a lot of autonomy and makes her feel appreciated. Her work environment is also fun and vibrant. 'When I came here for my interview, a guy walked past me in the lobby carrying a giant inflatable prawn. Any organisation that has the sense of humour to produce something like that is a place where I want to work,' she says.

It occurs to me that it isn't so much that Kelly loves her job; it is more that she loves her life, and her job is one element in her rich life.

Maybe when your life is enriched with other things, like hobbies, friends and family, then you can afford to lower your expectations of work, because your needs are being met in other ways.

When I chose to abandon my hobbies and put other aspects of my life on the back-burner while I pursued my career, it's no wonder that I ended up discontented and bitter. How could any job possibly fulfil my needs in every aspect of my life?

My friend Sue suggests that I try volunteering. She is a high-powered advertising executive who used to live and breathe her work. As a workaholic, she had long ago given up her passion for cycling, she couldn't fit a relationship into her schedule and could barely make time to return her friends' phone calls. She constantly wore an expression that said 'I'm too busy and far too important to talk to you right now.' Then one day she had a meltdown and her frustration turned to tears. She started crying and then kept on crying. She had the classic sobbing-on-the-bathroom-tiles moment and realised it was time to make some changes.

After some painful self-reflection and some self-help courses, Sue realised that she had lost perspective in her life. 'My whole life had been about me and proving myself,' she says. 'I realised there were bigger problems in the world than my day at work.'

Sue wanted to do something to give back to the community, so she volunteered with a local organisation that promotes reading to children. 'Its premise is that if children are read 1,000 books then they will become literate,' she says. 'If a kid starts school without exposure to books, she can never catch up.'

Sue chose to become a volunteer reader because she is passionate about education. 'I was able to break out of poverty because of the opportunities education provided me,' she says.

But Sue warns me that volunteering is not what she had expected. She had wanted it to be a really beautiful experience, but a lot of the time it is just frustrating and hard work. Sometimes the kids are little shits or the parents don't appreciate what she's doing. 'A lot of the time there is no warm glow,' she says. 'But I soon realised that it's not about me; it's about the child.'

A lot of career-guidance books suggest volunteering as a way of gaining new experiences and perspective. They say that most volunteers claim to learn more than they teach. Sue says that the kind of selflessness required to go back each week has been a big learning curve for her. She has a healthier perspective about her own life and also feels enriched by doing something that matters. 'This is my passion, and I want to make a difference to the world,' she says.

Inspired by Sue, Emma signs up with an organisation that provides temporary homes for the pets of abused women who are in crisis accommodation. Apparently one of the biggest reasons women don't leave abusive relationships is their fear of what might happen to their pets. There is crisis accommodation for women and children fleeing an abusive relationship, but it's not possible for them to take their pets. The idea is that women will be more inclined to leave a dangerous situation if they know their pets will also be safe. Emma offers to care for dogs, cats and rabbits. Despite her good intentions, she can't bring herself to care for snakes.

Chris suggests that I volunteer as a mentor to young women. I could use my people-management and business skills to help young women with their careers. He thinks that if I am working with people who haven't had the career opportunities that I've enjoyed I might get some perspective about my own job. I do a bit of Internet research and find two possibilities. One programme involves mentoring women from disadvantaged backgrounds who want to start their own businesses and the other aims to provide at-risk girls with a positive role model and some emotional support. Feeling wholesome and altruistic, I register with both programmes, but in both cases I'm told I have been added to the waiting list. Apparently there are more mentors than people who need mentoring. The estimated waiting list for both programmes is between six and twelve months. It seems I'm not the only jaded, discontented 30-something trying to do something that matters.

10

THE GLORIOUS SEVENTH DAY

Despite Emma's best efforts to become a volunteer, she is not called upon to assist. It seems there is an oversupply of crisis animal accommodation as well as mentors. So Emma continues to plug her existential void with booze and boys. I stop lecturing her about her irresponsible behaviour, because I am hardly a pin-up girl for a healthy lifestyle. I'm so disappointed by my lack of progress in solving my thrisis that I begin to let my frustration, cynicism and lethargy manifest itself in drinking gin every night, alternating between chocolate and ice cream as my staple food source and generally living like a slob. I spend every night in front of the television and won't even get off the couch to walk Toffee. The misery of work starts to leak into the rest of my life.

Chris sits me down one night for a bit of tough love. 'I'm worried about you, puss cat,' he says. 'The pattern has started again, and we both know where it leads.'

'What pattern?' I say defensively.

'The one where you stop looking after yourself,' he says. 'I haven't seen you eat a vegetable in weeks. All your clothes are strewn all over the apartment; you've stopped cooking . . .'

I cut him off and snap back, 'Oh, so this is about gender roles, is it? You expect me to cook for you.'

Chris's face is a mixture of alarm and amusement, and I feel ashamed. Chris is the last man on earth you could ever accuse of being sexist. He ignores my remark and continues. 'I don't mind cooking for you, though at the moment you're not even eating it,' he says. 'And I don't mind cleaning up after you or washing your clothes. But I worry about your lack of agency.'

I know where this conversation is going, and, as much as I don't want to hear it, I know that he's right. Letting myself go is the canary in the mine of my depression.

I need to break the cycle before things get out of control.

After my mother's attempt at suicide, I was diagnosed with Post-Traumatic Stress Disorder (PTSD). That, coupled with the breakdown of my family and the departure of my ex-boyfriend, threw me into a pit of depression. I'd then spent two years and a small fortune on therapy clawing my way out of it, so I can't allow myself to slip back down. I view depression as a bit like alcoholism or anorexia – once you've had it, it will always be a part of you.

Feeling 'over it' and depression are not the same things. While I am feeling discontented, frustrated and lethargic at the moment, I'm not depressed – yet. Having suffered from depression I can promise you that these feelings are not even on the same scale, but I do believe that one can lead to the other. Depression is like walking around in a heavy grey cloud and no matter what you do the sun can never shine through. It's a life without laughter, without music, without seasons and without hope. I feel like the black dog is always lurking around the corner and with a few bad choices it could be snapping at my heels again. I need to lift my game.

Chris talks me into doing a 12-week intensive fitness programme. It comes with exercise plans, meal plans and whole lot of protein bars, powders and other supplements. I am a little disconcerted by all the plastic-looking people on the website – there is way too much waxing, spray tanning and oiling going on for my liking.

The photos remind me of an ex-boyfriend who was a body-building champion. I don't know what I was thinking when I dated him; I suppose I was just flattered that he was interested in me, and he promised to teach me how to drive a car. It didn't last long, mostly because he was more interested in his own body than mine (and I got my licence). Poor guy, there wasn't much up top, or down below, for that matter. You know what they say about the side-effects of steroids? It's true.

As per the instructions, Chris and I take 'before' photos of ourselves in our underwear. Chris already looks hot, but as for me, let's just say that my diet of gin and chocolate has taken its toll.

The weekly exercise programme consists of three days of weights and three days of cardio. The cardio is only twenty minutes of interval training on the treadmill, but two minutes into it I feel like I'm going to die. I have a long way to go before I will be worthy of an 'after' photo.

The seventh day is my favourite day – there is no exercise, and we are allowed to eat whatever we want. In fact, the programme encourages people to eat pizza, cake, chips – you name it. The theory behind it is that your body will be so shocked by the contrast from the strict diet of cottage cheese and protein shakes from the previous six days that it will go into overdrive and kick-start your metabolism. Finally, I have something to look forward to again – the glorious seventh day!

It is all going well until week five. I wake up one morning with lower back pain. I dismiss it, assuming I've just overdone it on the back extensions the day before. By lunchtime, I've lost feeling in the toes of my left foot. Two hours later, my whole foot is numb. Not long after, the fingers on my left hand start tingling. When my fingers start turning blue, I panic.

Chris picks me up from work and takes me to hospital. The emergency department is bursting with bruised and bleeding people. I tell the triage nurse I've lost feeling down one side of my body and I am fast tracked through to see the doctor. I'll remember that for next time – present with stoke or heart attack symptoms and skip the queue.

Doctor Charlie is fresh out of medical school, can't quite grow a beard yet, and his voice breaks when he speaks. He does countless tests that include sticking pins in my feet and testing my reflexes with a hammer. His bedside manner could do with some work, especially when he casually remarks that it is possible I have a degenerative brain disease. He takes some blood and sends me back out to the waiting room to wait for the results.

I feel a little guilty when I sit next to a woman who has been waiting for over three hours. Comparatively, her complaint is minor. She *only* has deep vein thrombosis. Ruth is a flight attendant for a budget airline, and DVT is an occupational hazard. She says that she can never work again as a flight attendant. I tell Ruth that I am sorry to hear this. She laughs and says she is relieved – she is tired of cleaning up bodily fluids. At least once a week, Ruth has a passenger jerking off in his seat, and she has to get the captain to come out of the cockpit to tell the passenger to put it away.

I can't believe it. I've flown a lot in my life and not once have I ever seen a person servicing himself in the seat next to me. She says it happens all the time, especially on long-haul flights. Passengers also pee in the air-sick bags instead of getting up to go to the bathroom. They then leave the bags under the seat and the flight attendants have to clean them up. Flying will never be the same for me again.

DVT and cleaning up cum. My job isn't looking so bad after all.

After about half an hour, I go back in to see Charlie to get my blood-test results. The blood work is clear, so he sends me home with a referral for X-rays the following day. Despite numerous scans, the doctors still can't find anything wrong with me. I wonder if this incident is a metaphor for my 30-something discontent. Will I search and search for a cure to my thrisis only to be told that there is nothing wrong with me?

Over the next couple of weeks, the feeling in my hand and foot slowly returns. I wonder if my passion for work will one day do the same.

I decide that an extreme exercise programme is a health hazard, so I quit and reacquaint myself with my old friends – chocolate and cake. Although, the programme did succeed in breaking my downward cycle. I am being far healthier than I was prior to starting it.

The visit to the hospital makes me wonder if I'd be happier if I had a more meaningful job – like diagnosing a degenerative brain disease or writing out referrals for X-rays.

My friend Robert has changed quite a bit since he's become a doctor. We became friends as teenagers, and I take credit for teaching him how to kiss. Strangely, his wife has never thanked me for this service. He is much more composed and controlled than he was when we were younger. He tells me that I would change too if every day at work a person that I said hello to in the morning was dead by the time I was sugaring my afternoon latte.

I have a lot more sympathy and respect for doctors now that Robert and some of my other friends have sworn their Hippocratic oath. There is no question about the meaning in the job of a doctor; however, that meaning comes at a price. Take mistakes for example. When a doctor stuffs up, they can kill someone. When I used to hear stories of doctor error, I'd only think about the patient and their family and curse the incompetent doctor. Now I think about the poor doctor who did something inevitable for a human – made a mistake – and now has to live with knowing for the rest of his life that he killed somebody. A friend of mine told me when she was doing her intern year it wasn't a question of *if* she and the other junior doctors killed somebody, it was *when*. Apparently the rate of 'negative patient outcomes' in hospitals increases every year when the new doctors start.

Doctors always have to be 'on'. They can't spend all day having coffees and long lunches or reading their online horoscope, the way I am spending my days at the moment. I suppose there are a lot of jobs like this: police officers, pilots, nurses, barristers. If barristers make mistakes or spend all day surfing the net instead of doing their job, somebody could end up in jail.

I like to think I'm pretty good at my job, but I stuff up all the time. I've made some monumental stuff-ups in my time. The worst mistake I ever made at work was hiring a guy who used to be in the

Israeli army. He was a real hothead, and I found out later that some of my female colleagues were scared of him. I gave him a job because I felt sorry for him. He'd just arrived back in the country after doing his time in the army and needed a break. Things were rocky from the start, but in the beginning it was at least tolerable to have him around – that was until the day somebody left a briefcase in reception. Bear in mind that this was the 1990s – long before 9/11 and way before we would look twice at an unattended briefcase. However, fresh out of military service, Army-boy assumed the briefcase was a bomb and proceeded to evacuate the building – all 35 floors. It didn't occur to him to call security or even the police; he simply went from floor to floor evacuating everyone. That afternoon, my manager intervened and sacked him. My manager also banned me from hiring any more staff. It's interesting how times have changed. If something like that happened now, Army-boy would probably be lauded as a hero. Although, not everything has changed; I still tend to make really bad recruitment decisions.

In the past, when I made mistakes at work I used to take it to heart and feel sick to my stomach. Now I take it much more in my stride. Stuffing up doesn't affect me as much as it used to because I've realised the consequences of my mistakes – almost zero. If I make a mistake, I might delay a project by a couple of weeks or lose some money for somebody who already has enough. Or, the most likely scenario is that nobody will even notice – the way nobody notices that I spend half my day at the pet shop.

When nobody knows or cares about the mistakes you make at work, you can't help but feel irrelevant.

11

HEADHUNTING

My Internet surfing is interrupted by a phone call. It is a private number so I let it go to voice mail. I'm always suspicious of people who block their numbers. I assume they are either paranoid security freaks or trying to sell me something.

I am right: it is a headhunter trying to sell me on a new job. Annabel's message says I've been highly recommended and she'd like to speak to me about an opportunity as a senior change management consultant for a world-leading IT company. Great – the same boring, meaningless shit, only with a different logo on my business card. I don't return her call.

She calls again a few days later. This time I answer and because I don't have anything better to do I agree to meet with her. I am pretty sure I'm not going to be interested in what she has to say, but it's always nice to get a free coffee and an ego stroking.

If I were to tell you what I really think, I'd tell you that I believe all headhunters are scumbags. They are ruthless, insincere and just plain liars – they're your best friend until you sign the contract. Once the ink has dried, they discard you and move on to the next host body to support their parasitic existence. But since I like to hide my harsh, judgemental side from people for as long as possible, let's just say that when it comes to morality and ethics, I believe most headhunters have room for improvement.

So imagine my surprise when I meet one that isn't a scumbag. Annabel surprises me. She appears to be genuine and possess the rare trait of integrity. Surely that's a liability in her industry? I click with her straight away, so when she tells me about the job opportunity I push my cynicism into the background and give her the benefit of the doubt.

She asks me if I've ever considered working for ABC Company (the name of the company has been changed to protect the innocent, and my career). I say no, and she looks surprised. This is one of the largest and most prestigious software companies in the world. She tells me that people are queuing to get in. They have won employer of choice awards and have a female chief executive officer. On that basis alone, I agree to go along to an interview to meet the head of business consulting.

Over the weekend, I do some research about the company. The more I read, the more interested I become – it is big, rich, innovative, multinational and promises that it is a 'place to grow' for employees. Maybe it will provide me with the intellectual challenge I've been craving.

The day before the interview, my father calls to invite me to his wedding. Things have been pretty rocky between us since he left my mother, mostly because I was in the frontline and experienced all the pain and suffering he had left behind. But time has passed, and I desperately want to restore my relationship with him. I miss him. So even though watching my dad marry another woman will be bizarre and confronting, I want to be there as a gesture of my acceptance and support. I say yes.

Four hours later, my father phones back to dis-invite me to his wedding. Is 'dis-invite' even a word in the English language? Maybe we don't need a word for it because it's such a cruel and hurtful thing to do that people don't do it.

I can only assume he'd invited me without consulting his partner, and once she found out she vetoed it. He tells me he doesn't want me to attend because I'm not nice to his partner. I am crushed by the injustice. If I were a bitch to his partner then, OK, he'd be justified in his accusation. But the thing is, I've tried. I've really tried. The last time I saw them I even gave her a pair of earrings as a gift. They were nice too, and expensive. If I'd known she would still find reason to dislike me, I would have kept them for myself.

Admittedly in the beginning I was wary of her, but for over a year I've tried all sorts of things to demonstrate my acceptance. The truth is, I actually like her. I also like how happy she makes my dad. I even went so far as telling them straight out that I was happy for them both. Apparently they doubted my sincerity.

The thing is, if I wanted to be a bitch I could have been. The injustice of being unfairly accused is almost unbearable. I can't tell you how devastated I am by my father's accusations and invitation revocation. I find out later from another relative that my father is worried that if I go to the wedding I'd ruin the day for everybody. I can't imagine what he thinks I might do. And I can't understand how he can have such a low opinion of me.

This is a defining moment in my life. Just as my illusions of work and organisations shattered when I became 30-something and over it, so too have my last remaining illusions about my family. The two institutions through which I previously derived my identity and sense of self-worth have crumbled around me. At a rational level, I know that my shattered illusions will make it easier to follow my brother Michael's advice about rejecting society's expectations and carving out my own path. But that doesn't make my grief any less painful.

I cry all night and into the morning. I am still crying on the way to my interview at ABC Company. Thank God for waterproof mascara and concealer.

Even though I am impressed by the vision and passion of the head of business consulting who interviews me, my heart isn't in it. I am speaking words about change management, but all I can think about is my irreparable relationship with my dad. Despite all my professional achievements and all the things I have done to try to make my father proud of me, I'm still not good enough. This realisation makes the desire to claw my way up the corporate ladder seem even more ridiculous. If it doesn't make me happy, and it doesn't make my father accept me, who am I doing it for, and why?

I am pretty sure my interview performance isn't good enough either, so I prepare myself for the 'thanks but no thanks' phone call. Imagine my surprise when Annabel phones a few days later to tell me that I've got through to the second-round interview. The interviewer was impressed by my 'relaxed style'. Can you believe it? I wasn't relaxed; I was disillusioned, devastated, rejected and over it. Who would have thought that losing my give-a-shit, and my dad, could be so good for my career?

Chris takes me out for a drink to celebrate my interview success, and we start up a conversation with two women at the bar. They are in their late 30s and look expensive in their charcoal suits and white-gold accessories. Judy tells us that she loves her job. She works in sales and says it's really satisfying to close a deal. Her husband stays at home to look after their two kids while she works. She wouldn't have it any other way. In fact, even though she loves her kids and would never give them back, she says that if she had her time over again she wouldn't have them.

I am amazed to hear her say this. Never in my life have I heard a mother say this about her children. I'm ashamed to admit it, but my social conditioning about how mothers can and cannot feel about motherhood is so strong that the first thought that pops into my head is 'You monster'. However, from what I can tell on first meeting her, Judy is not a monster and she's probably a damn good mother. How dare I judge her for being honest? I wonder how many other mothers feel the same as Judy but dare not speak of it for fear of being judged. Imagine the guilt they must carry around with them.

To my surprise, Judy's friend Samantha says, 'Well, since we're being honest, I feel the same way.' Samantha says she much preferred her life before she had children and she can't wait until they are older so she can go back to work full-time.

I am impressed by Judy and Samantha's honesty. It is hugely

courageous for them to admit that they would have preferred a different path. It's not so surprising when I think about it. People are different, so it's ridiculous to assume that we would all share the same views on motherhood, or anything else for that matter.

These conversations make me think about my own situation. Just as it is socially unacceptable for women to admit they would have preferred not to have children, it is also socially unacceptable for somebody with a good job to admit they don't want it. Barbara Sher says she feels sorry for people with high-paying, high-status jobs, because unlike other people who are allowed to complain about their rotten situations, '"Lucky" Fast Trackers . . . think they've got the brass ring so they don't have the right to complain. But they're looking around bewildered – trying to figure out what went wrong.'

I realise that being 30-something and over it is taboo.

12

OPTING OUT

The 'opt-out generation' disagree with Judy and Samantha.

I discover the phrase 'opt-out generation' one day at work when I am Googling. It was born when *New York Times* journalist Lisa Belkin sent her feminist sisters into a tailspin by writing about affluent, educated women who *choose* to abandon the workforce in preference of family life and motherhood.

These are the women who graduated top of their classes and have the potential to claw their way further up the corporate ladder than any women in history. They should be making their revolutionary sisters weep with pride, but instead of running companies and ruling countries they say, 'Fuck it, I'd rather stay home and watch *The Tweenies*.'

Belkin posed the question 'Why don't women rule the world?', and then she both outraged and liberated women everywhere with the answer, 'because they don't want to'.

As I read these words, I feel like I've been released from bondage – as in that experienced by the Israelites, not the type of bondage my brother Michael recommends. I don't want to rule the world either. Well, not any more. But I'd never dared to think it, let alone say it.

On the last day of high school, my teacher asked everyone in the class what we saw ourselves doing in ten to fifteen years' time. When she came around to me, I said, 'Married with kids and a stay-at-home mother.' The teacher and the class burst into laughter, and so did I. It was obvious to everyone I was just being a smartarse. It wasn't just me that expected I would end up a high-powered woman in either corporate or civic life; everyone else did too. Why else would my parents have paid for two sets of braces and public-speaking lessons?

Later, a classmate confessed to me that she did actually want to be 'just' a mother. She looked ashamed, and I looked indignant. What a waste of a good education.

I'm ashamed to reveal that even as a teenager I was guilty of participating in the mummy wars and judging another woman for her mothering preferences. It seems that stay-at-home mothers are still being accused of being anti-feminist and poor role models to their daughters, whereas working mothers have been accused of everything from child abuse to being selfish feminists and inflating housing prices. Women are pitched against other women, and no matter where you stand in this minefield you can't help but notice that men seem to escape the guilt and the blame.

Leora Tanenbaum, author of *Catfight*, believes that men are the beneficiaries of the debate. 'With mothers under constant scrutiny, fathers, by and large, escape judgement of any kind,' she says.

Tanenbaum believes that the mummy wars have become so vicious because women feel insecure and competitive about their mothering skills and decisions, largely because mothers seem to be blamed for most of society's problems. And as long as mothers alone are held responsible for raising well-adjusted children the viciousness will continue.

I'm not a parent, so I don't feel qualified to weigh into the debate – but I'm not going to let that stop me! Surely good mothers are happy mothers? What I can say with some authority is that when you're depressed you can't even take care of yourself, let alone be physically and emotionally available for a child. So forcing mothers into lifestyles that don't make them happy, or judging and blaming those who dare not to conform, is bad for everyone – for the mother, the baby, the partner and society. Even Oliver James, who championed the merits of stay-at-home mothering in his book *Affluenza*, concedes that it's better to have a working mother with good mental health than a full-time mother with depression or anxiety.

The idea that there is only one correct formula for motherhood is not only ridiculous, it's cruel. Surely motherhood is hard enough as it is without people laying more guilt and blame on mothers. My colleague Melissa tells me that no matter what a woman decides to do, motherhood is guilt.

It's also a shame that while we are caught in the eternal loop of arguing about stay-at-home mothering versus working motherhood, we are distracting ourselves from potentially more fruitful debates such as fathers sharing more of the parenting responsibilities, better child-care options and the inflexibility of the workplace that by its very nature discriminates against mothers.

Despite the inevitable guilt of motherhood, I find myself each morning on the train to work fantasising about having a baby – not because I particularly want a bundle of joy of my very own but because I wouldn't have to show up to work any more. Even ambitious and driven Karen from the strategic management consulting company had considered motherhood as an express route out of the rat race.

I know how extreme it sounds to even contemplate having a child for these reasons. I've heard my mother tell me time and time again that raising a child is the hardest thing you'll ever do (and the most rewarding, she adds, when I look hurt and dejected).

One of the attractions I see of motherhood is that it would give me a non-negotiable, non-refundable baby. I'm talking about my friend Godfrey's metaphorical baby theory – something to focus on, invest in and worry about for the next 20 years. It would open up the next pathway in life that I could follow without question. It would give me purpose and meaning – not to mention the sleep deprivation, stretch marks and school fees.

I think there is something to be said for the restrictions placed on you as a parent. According to a lot of the 'happiness literature', it's the abundance of choice that is making us unhappy. From what I can see, having kids diminishes your range of choices.

Susan Maushart in *What Women Want Next* says that 'the responsibility for making the right choices used to lie with our fathers, husbands and churches. We now have the freedom to choose our life path, but we also have the anxiety and guilt which go with it.'

In *The Paradox of Choice*, author Barry Schwartz takes it one step further by suggesting that the multitude of options and choices may be the real cause of the dramatic increase in clinical depression in the developed world.

It's not just about choosing between being a career woman or a mother, or even trying to be both; when I read books like *What Color is Your Parachute?* or *Be What You Are*, I'm overwhelmed by the possibilities within the possibilities. And I hate the brutal reality that if I make the wrong choice, or even not the best choice, I have nobody to blame but myself.

But having said that, I do feel lucky that I at least have the freedom to search for and hopefully choose what I love, in a way that my grandmother did not – if she didn't love being a wife and a mother, then that would have been tough luck, sista. It wasn't a matter of her not finding her passion; there simply wasn't one to be found.

When I think about my grandmother's lack of opportunities, I feel like such a spoilt brat. I have career opportunities that my grandmother's generation couldn't even dream of and for which my mother's generation burned their bras. And yet at the moment, when I think of realising the career opportunities that these generations made possible for me, I'd rather stick a pencil in my eye.

I wonder if this is one of the reasons why being 30-something and over it is taboo? When you've been given a gift that has been handcrafted for over 40 years, it feels rude and ungrateful not to accept it. On the other hand, Virginia Haussegger, who wrote *Wonder Woman: The Myth of Having It All*, wonders if the gift has an exchange receipt. She feels foolish for taking the word of her feminist foremothers as gospel and for believing that 'female fulfilment came with a leather briefcase'.

Virginia Haussegger is in good company. The research organisation Catalyst found that 26 per cent of women at the cusp of the most senior levels of management don't want to be promoted. Emma just turned down a promotion in her organisation. She says she just can't be bothered – and neither can the other three women in her team who were all asked to fill the role and all said no. It would have been too much time, too much stress and too much effort pushing 'shit up-hill', and she's seen what happened to the woman who previously held the role. 'She was a complete mess by the time she left,' Emma says. 'It impacted on her health and her relationship, and I thought, "What part of that appeals to me?" Her life there was hell. She wasn't listened to or supported, and then when she got frustrated and responded emotionally she became like an injured lamb in a lions' den.' Emma says that the only thing the woman did wrong was not being male enough. She didn't play the game.

Emma has also realised that there are a lot of deadshits above her. 'I don't want to be one of them,' Emma says. 'They're fuckwits. And when I think about how they got to those positions I know it must have been the wrong way. It couldn't possibly have been based on their performance, because they're just not very good.'

Susan Pinker suggests in *The Sexual Paradox* that another reason women turn down promotions is because they suffer from the impostor syndrome. Despite their experience, rank, salary and past success, many women believe that they are phonies. They attribute their previous accomplishments to nothing more than luck and live in fear that their incompetence will be discovered. Because of the self-doubt, they either turn down opportunities or don't nominate themselves in the first place. Pinker quotes Valerie Young, an expert on the impostor syndrome, who says, 'Men are more comfortable bluffing. Before women will apply for a job or raise their hand, they feel they have to know 100 per cent, whereas men feel they only have to know 50 per cent and can fake the rest.'

Over the years, I've become better at overcoming it, but I am also frequently plagued by the impostor syndrome. It started long before

I hit the workforce. When I was 12 years old, I cried myself to sleep night after night because everybody thought I was clever but I knew that I really wasn't. I had buckled under the burden of this deception, and the more my mother tried to assure me that I was smart, the more burdened I felt. Even as I type these words, I can't help but think 'Who am I to write a book? Who could possibly be interested in anything I have to say?'

Most of the time I can overcome my impostor syndrome by convincing myself that everyone is an impostor to some degree. As I said before, I honestly believe that most people are faking it at work. So I bolster my confidence by telling myself that if everyone else is faking it then surely I can too.

Clearly we don't all suffer from it to the same degree. Emma was anxious for the first few months when she was promoted to the executive team because there was at least a ten-year gap between her and the next nearest person and she was the only woman. But, 'Even if I was insecure for a short time, I always knew I was smarter than half of them anyway,' she says. 'Maybe I have that chromosome disorder that is XXY – mostly woman but part man.'

Susan Maushart in *What Women Want Next* writes that despite the progress our mothers and grandmothers made in creating opportunities for women in the workplace, what many of us would prefer from work seems to be less of it. 'Playing hardball looked so thrilling when we watched from the sidelines. Up close and personal, it's a game we're not even sure we want to play, let alone win. And as far as taking men as our role models, let's just be polite and say that most of us want less of that as well.'

The issue is so widespread that governments, law firms, banks and large corporations are so concerned about their inability to retain top women that they are commissioning studies into the subject. Mary Lou Quinlan, former CEO of a New York advertising agency, famously said: 'It's not about talent, dedication, experience or the ability to take the heat. Women simply say, "I just don't like that kitchen."'

Nevertheless, I can't help but wonder if Lisa Belkin only told half the story. I completely understand that mothers would want to give up their careers to focus on their families – especially when you read statistics that suggest women in paid work still perform roughly two-thirds of all household labour. Working motherhood is a tough gig. But I wonder, maybe women aren't opting out of the workforce because they want babies; perhaps they're having babies because they want to opt out of the workforce? My friend Sara, a lawyer who has recently become a mother, says to me: 'Have a baby, Kase. It's the only socially acceptable reason to give up work.'

Becoming a mother has changed the way Sara views work. She doesn't necessarily want to be a full-time mother for ever, but she wants to make sure that any work she does is meaningful to her as well as others. 'I've realised that it just isn't worth sacrificing so much of my child's life for a job that isn't particularly fulfilling.'

I ask around to find other women who have changed their views on working since they've had kids. Annabel the headhunter introduces me to her friend Rosemary who has strong views on the subject. Rosemary is vivacious, fun and razor sharp. She's one of those people who have the unique gift of using obscenities in a way that enhances the language rather than just making things sound base or crude. When I meet her, she is wearing a purple faux-fur coat, and I like her immediately. It's not every day you meet someone who has the confidence to wear a Muppet and the style to pull it off.

She's just turned 40 and is lamenting the fact that her life isn't how she thought it would be when she hit 40. 'I wanted to be thinner and have my house paid off,' she says as she laughs, pats her thighs (which are not fat) and orders the pasta marinara with the cream sauce.

She has a couple of kids and a husband at home while she works on large-scale software implementations. Working in IT, Rosemary has the greater earning potential, which is why she wins the bread while her husband stays home with the kids. Her husband has embraced the role of stay-at-home parent and recently thanked her for giving him the opportunity to look after the kids as well as enabling him to opt out of an unsatisfying and stressful career.

Before Rosemary had kids she used to care a lot about her work. She'd stay late at night, work weekends and continually stress about her performance. But now her job is just a source of income. 'I'm a whore. I only work for the money,' she says. 'If the IT system crashed, I used to take it so seriously; now, I don't give a fuck. If somebody flips out because the server is down, I think, "So what? Last night my kid had a fever."'

Because she doesn't have the luxury of opting out, she recently tried to find more meaningful work doing something else. She looked into other options such as being a guidance counsellor in schools, but after she discovered how poorly they were paid she realised she couldn't afford to be anything other than a corporate soldier.

Talking to Rosemary is a bit of a reality check for my fantasy of using motherhood as a ticket off the treadmill. Given my dismal financial situation, having a kid won't liberate me from the workforce; it will only tighten the shackles, and for longer. I'm even more surprised and dismayed to read in both Susan Pinker and Leora Tanenbaum's books that studies have shown that mothers who work are happier, and thinner, than those who don't. Jennie Bristow writes in *Spiked Online*: 'Maternity leave is still considered as something of a perk to be enjoyed by women of a certain age – a part-funded gap year enabling endless lie-ins, domestic goddessry and bonding with one's precious infant. Those of us who have been there might point out that the reality is rather less pleasant, involving lunatic bouts of sleep deprivation and hands raw from mopping up sick.'

I begin to realise that popping out a baby is not the quick fix I was hoping it would be. I think Chris is pleased with this realisation – I don't think he's quite ready to turn our study into the baby's room.

13

DICKLESS

I've come to the conclusion that it doesn't matter if women have children or don't have children, nor does it matter if they want them or they don't, it seems women everywhere are over it.

I email Susan Maushart, the author of *What Women Want Next*, to get her take on the situation, and she replies with: 'I'm wondering whether the loss of give-a-shit is evidence of being a more evolved soul, or just a profoundly disillusioned one. Or maybe the one simply implies the other!'

Everywhere I look, I see women with evolved and disillusioned souls. When I tell them how I am feeling, I can see the relief on their faces – as if I've just given them permission to admit they are feeling the same way. It makes me wonder how many other people are suffering in silence – showing up to work each day with smiles on their faces when they are shrivelling up on the inside.

I wonder if it is just women who have lost their give-a-shit or if men feel the same. It seems to me that women are more discontented than men, but maybe men are just better at hiding their discontent. Barbara Sher believes it affects both sexes. In *I Could Do Anything, If I Only Knew What It Was*, she claims that 98 per cent of Americans are unhappy in their jobs. Holy shit! Is the problem really that universal? Why hasn't the revolution started yet?

But on the other hand, a study by the Australian Social Policy

Research Centre claims that 82 per cent of men who are able to work part-time or are eligible for other family-friendly work arrangements choose not to take advantage of them. Does this imply that men are simply into work in a way that women are not?

Susan Pinker believes this is the case. In *The Sexual Paradox*, she refers to a number of studies that have demonstrated that women are far more motivated by intrinsic goals, such as making a difference and belonging to a community, than extrinsic goals. Men are more motivated by the extrinsic goals of money, power and status. So it's fair to say that most workplaces support what men want and conflict with what women want. She also adds that when a man takes parental leave, he doesn't necessarily use the time for parenting, quoting a junior university professor: 'A woman takes family leave and comes back with a backlog, a man takes family leave and comes back with a book.'

Susan Pinker explains the gender difference with biology. She claims that women are wired differently from men and therefore want meaning and fulfilment in their work, whereas men are sustained by the prospect of competing and winning. When women try to squeeze themselves into workplaces and cultures that are set up by men to support men, it's no wonder they feel like they don't fit. I relate to Susan's theory. In my 20s, I contorted myself to mimic the male model and sometimes I even pushed back on the rigid constraints naively hoping I could change them. But after a decade of little success, I'm just over it.

Susan Pinker writes: 'Most of us don't realise that we think of male as the standard, and of female as a version of this base model – with just a few optional features added on.' She says we expect that for women to be equal they should be like men, but this is at odds with our nature.

But I can't agree with Pinker when she uses her biological argument to downplay discrimination as the cause for women's stifled careers. She says that the absence of women at the top of companies does not indicate discrimination, because women are *choosing* to opt out of the workplace or refusing to take promotions because of conflicts with their values or their family responsibilities. But if workplaces are set up to support the biological and social needs of men and do not accommodate the needs of women, isn't this also discrimination? When it's mothers and not fathers who are unable to take a promotion because of family responsibilities, or who stunt their career by working part-time, surely this is discrimination as well? In some cases it's organisations who are discriminating against women; in other cases it's husbands and fathers who are not carrying their share of the domestic load, but there is no denying that women, particularly mothers, face discrimination.

UK columnist Camilla Cavendish wrote in *The Times* that her friends who are combining work and motherhood share a common fear of promotion. She says that while many women are reluctant to admit it, their lives are such a complex balancing act that any extra responsibility at work could tip them over the edge.

And I simply don't buy the argument that if a woman chooses to have children then she and she alone should suffer the consequences of the break to her career, the loss of income and status, and the stress of juggling a career and a family. It pisses me off when people say, 'I didn't have a child, so why should my taxes pay for it?', or, 'I can't leave at 5 p.m. to pick up the kids, so why should you?' Governments all over the developed world are worried about negative birth rates, so much so that the Australian government, for example, is paying women an incentive bonus to have children. Society needs children: we need them to grow up and pay taxes to fund our retirement and our hip replacements. Companies also need children. Companies need children to grow up and buy things to keep the economy going, but yet they are unwilling to make the necessary workplace changes to support the mothers of these children. As Susan Pinker says: 'Nonpartnership tracks, part-time and flexitime are often code words for a dead end to your career.'

While mothers often can't work long hours, non-mothers in general don't want to either. One of the biggest differences I notice between men and women on the work-satisfaction issue is the way we feel about working long hours. There is a general consensus among the women I speak with that they simply don't want to work the long hours any more, particularly those women who have children. They resent that work has become so invasive that even when they are not at the office they are still expected to be 'on', still expected to answer their mobile phone, pick up emails and attend out-of-hours networking functions. The author of *Get a New Life*, Kaye Fallick, says that trying to make the distinction between your work life and the rest is 'like trying to remove the flour from the cake once it has been baked'.

But many of the men I know seem to get off on the fact that they work long hours: it seems to make them feel important and indispensable. One of my male friends makes a point of telling me every time I see him that he's expecting an important call which he'll have to take. He places his Blackberry in a conspicuous place on the table and constantly monitors it as if it's the Bat Phone. How important can somebody be that they can't even have coffee with a friend without having to take a call?

Even though women resent working long hours, so many of us still do it. I used to be a regular offender but now cringe when I hear people make a point of telling anybody who will listen that they worked at the weekend, as if it's an achievement rather than a symptom of warped priorities. I sit next to a woman who is forever on the phone saying, 'I don't have time to look at it today, but I'll work on it tonight', or, 'I'll work on it at the weekend.' Then she'll get off the phone all stressed and frustrated and bemoan the fact that she has no life.

One day, I ask her what would be the consequence of saying no and explaining that she doesn't have the time. Or of telling them that she'll do it the next day or even the next week? I've been applying this strategy for months now, and I can honestly say that there are no consequences. In fact, Lois Frankel from *Nice Girls Don't Get The Corner Office* says that taking on work like this is a massive career-limiting mistake. It gives the impression that you can't stand up for yourself or that you're inefficient. But the workaholic sitting next to me sees it differently. She says, 'If I don't do it, somebody else will, and I'll be out of a job.'

I decide to speak to one of my male friends and colleagues to get his perspective on whether or not men are over it, too. Jamie is also a management consultant, working in the IT industry. He's driven, enthusiastic and committed, with a killer smile and an impressive tie collection. I envy the way he seems to whole-heartedly throw himself into work. He seems to care about it and enjoy it. I want to know his secret.

Over a glass of wine, I casually enquire, 'Jamie, do you ever feel like you don't want to work any more?' He looks at me bemused and then to my complete surprise says, 'All the time, mate.'

He says he only works because he has to pay the mortgage and support his family. He doesn't get the same buzz from climbing the corporate ladder that he did in his 20s, but he views working as a necessary part of life and therefore has resolved to make the best of it. 'There is no point to me moaning about having to go to work and making it miserable for myself and the people around me,' he says. 'So I make the most of it while I'm there and get fulfilment from other aspects of my life.'

The difference between Jamie and me, and many of the other women I've spoken to, is that Jamie seems resigned to his fate of corporate drudgery and is just getting on with it. On the other hand, my sisters and I are not so willing to accept unfulfilling work as our lot in life. We are resisting it, resenting it and dreaming about alternatives.

Just like Rodney, the consultant with the life-balance concentric circles, Jamie has much lower expectations about work than I have. Neither of them seems to yearn for the sense of meaning the way I do, and they seem a lot happier about the prospect of showing up to work five days a week for the next thirty years.

I decide to explore the gender difference with another man and send an email to Nigel Marsh, author of *Fat, Forty and Fired* and *Observations of a Very Short Man*. He graciously phones me to share his views on the subject.

Nigel Marsh is 40-something and over it, but, unlike a lot of the women I have been speaking with, he needed to lose his job before he reflected on his life. He says that if he hadn't lost his job he would have kept on keeping on. 'For men it takes a crisis for them to pause and think about their lives and whether or not they actually like what they are doing,' he says.

Marsh attributes the insight and perceptiveness of women to the fact that they have the option to leave the workforce to have children. 'Women have an in-built break in their careers that they don't have to feel embarrassed or guilty about,' he says. 'It's socially acceptable for women to take a break from work. Women have an enforced, natural and respectable opportunity to assess life and what they want from it.'

Marsh believes that it's different for men, because it's not cool or macho to stop and take stock of their lives and what's important to them. 'If you step off the treadmill, then people think you're soft or you can't hack it.'

It is weird to hear him say this. If I had the means to do so, I'd quit work tomorrow. I fantasise about it every day without fail. It hasn't once occurred to me that anybody would think that I am quitting because I can't hack it. In fact, in my mind I would be doing something brave and courageous.

Maybe women feel more dissatisfied than men because they are simply allowed to feel more in general. You don't need to read *Men are from Mars* and *Women Can't Read Maps* to know that men are discouraged from showing their emotions from a very young age in a way that women are not.

Searching for answers, I ask Emma why she thinks women seem more over it than men. 'Because we don't have dicks,' she says simply. 'By the time we get to our 30s we've realised that a dick is far more valuable in the workplace than intellect, education or dedication. We'll never have the necessary equipment.'

14

NICE GIRLS DON'T

On the very first day of Emma's very first job, her boss said to her, 'It's a shame you're not a boy. I tried to hire a bloke but couldn't find one, so I had to take you.'

Back then, Emma and I were both naive and idealistic enough to think that this was a freak occurrence. Surely the workplace wasn't like this any more? Surely the feminist movement had achieved more than this in almost half a century?

Early in her career, Emma tried to deal with the sexism by becoming one of the boys. She'd drink beers with them when it was declared 'pub o'clock', and she'd join in when the guys were picking on somebody in the lunch room. She became a master of practical jokes, locking one guy in a cupboard and freezing her boss's car keys in a block of ice so he couldn't go home until it melted. But getting too close to the boys meant that they'd just get drunk and try to crack onto her, and then she realised that she was never one of them at all.

'I don't have to deal with the day-to-day sexism any more, because it's illegal and people have to be so careful,' Emma says. 'Now it's become more subtle and insidious, like being the only one on the management team to be asked to take notes in the meetings or asked to pour the drinks.'

In my world of management consulting, however, the sexism is not so subtle. Last year, I was told by an account director that I couldn't manage a certain project because I was 'too young, too pretty and too female'. Shocking, I know – not to mention illegal. It seems the laws have changed over time but the reality has not. The worst part about the episode with the account director was that when I raised the issue with management they thought I should be flattered, as if I'd just been paid a personal compliment rather than a professional insult.

Let's face it: the progress in gender equity has been glacial. And we all know that sexual discrimination and sexual harassment didn't go away just because of legislation and lip service.

A few years ago, a male colleague told me that I got better clients than he did because I was blonde and had big tits. I let it slide because I knew that making any sort of complaint would hurt my career more than it would his. A few months later at a work function, the same colleague pinched my butt, grabbed my breasts and asked my boyfriend at the time if he'd lend me to him for sex. This time I did make a complaint. I was made to feel like I was over-reacting and the sleaze bag ended up being promoted into a position of leadership.

A senior woman in a professional services company was quoted in *BOSS Magazine* as saying that there is still an underlying belief among men in business that successful women got there by accident or a fluke in timing. When Annabel the headhunter told me that the chief executive officer of ABC Company was a female, I shouldn't have been impressed or surprised. Ideally, the gender of a CEO should be as unremarkable as their hair colour. But I am now well aware, as a result of bitter experience, that the playing field is far from level.

Emma says one of the biggest impediments to career advancement for women is that the women who can support us have left the workforce to have kids. 'All my mentors are no longer working,' she says. 'Sometimes when the right person says in the right meeting that you're a gun, it can change your career. Men will back their mates. Even if I did want a promotion, all the women who could possibly back me are at home with their kids.'

I worked out early on in my career that the best chance we have to get anywhere in this man's world is to be more like a man. Every time I walk through the door at work, I'm pretending – and I'm not just talking about over-inflating my skills and competencies; I don a pretend personality, too. I'm constantly role-playing Corporate Kasey – professional, serious, earnest and conservative. It's exhausting, and I'm not alone. According to a survey conducted by Hewlett-Packard and the Simmons School of Management, 89 per cent of women surveyed believe they have to do the same in order to succeed in the workplace.

I thought I had been doing a pretty good job at it until I read Lois Frankel's *Nice Girls Don't Get The Corner Office.* This book lists 100 things which women do in the workplace that sabotage their corporate image and consequently their career progression. I am amazed at how many career-limiting behaviours I display on a daily basis.

Cleaning up the kitchen is a big stumbling block. It seems that above every sink in every kitchen in every workplace in the world is a sign telling people to wash their own dishes and not leave them in the sink. Yet, without fail, in every workplace I've ever been in there are always dishes in the sink. Now I'm not a neat freak by any stretch of the imagination. My flat is almost always a disaster zone, and I am so lucky that Chris has one of the highest mess-thresholds known to man. But it makes me crazy that there seems to be an unwritten law that the more senior you are the more mess you can leave for other people to clean up: as if managers are too busy and too important to put their cups in the dishwasher. I pity their secretaries, not to mention their wives. No employee should ever have to wash up the lunchbox of their boss. It's a basic human right, surely? So at work not only do I always clean up after myself, I feel compelled to help out the poor receptionist or secretary who gets lumped with cleaning up everyone else's mess.

However, when reading Frankel's book I realise that cleaning up after other people will damage my personal 'brand'. I'll be seen as a subordinate rather than an equal. I start protecting 'brand me' by being as messy and selfish as my superiors and contemporaries. So now when I walk past the kitchen and see a mountain of dishes I look the other way and keep walking. On the outside I project my professional persona, but on the inside I feel like a selfish cow.

When I catch one of the women in my team packing the dishwasher, I demand she stop immediately, telling her she is doing a disservice to herself and the sisterhood. Now there are even more dishes piled in the kitchen for the receptionist to deal with and I feel even more selfish.

Because my Corporate Kasey persona is more serious, less honest, less emotional and a lot more male than I am in my natural state, it's a really hard balance to strike. If I'm too male, then I'll be labelled a hard-arsed bitch; but if I'm too soft, I'll be considered ineffectual. This level of inauthenticity is exhausting, and either way I know I'll never be considered to be as good as a man.

The prevalence of sex and porn in the workplace is another reason why women will be forever excluded. On a previous assignment, my desk was outside my client's office. I don't know whether he didn't realise I could see his computer screen or he just didn't care, but I watched him, day after day, surfing for porn. He had a thing for discipline. Not that I'm a prude – I used to live in Amsterdam and have been to more sex shows than I can count (I'll never forget the show with the gorilla suit, banana and vibrator . . . but that's another story), but objectifying women in the workplace, in my opinion, is totally unacceptable.

Another organisation I worked for regularly held meetings in strip clubs. Let me tell you, I've seen some tits and arse in my time. The first time it happened, I was truly shocked. Then I suppose I just got used to substituting the oak boardroom table for a different kind of tabletop.

I was working for a manufacturing client at the time and was the only woman on the project. At the last minute, the venue for the meeting was changed from the factory to a club in the city – apparently it was so we could have a 'working lunch'. It was interesting terminology, because it certainly wasn't sandwiches sitting on the table.

Can you imagine how distracting it was to discuss timelines and budgets while naked women gyrated on the table? I didn't know where to look – if I looked up, I felt like I was perving at the women's breasts and if I looked down, I felt like I was perving at my colleagues' erections. Another dilemma was whether or not I should tip. I wanted to tip big to support my sisters, and the corporate policy stated that we could claim tips as a legitimate business expense, but I was unsure where to put it. It didn't seem right to stick money in another woman's garter belt.

I didn't ever work out whether my colleagues decided to take me to strip clubs to shock and mock me or because they were just doing what they always did and they didn't concern themselves with how I might feel about it. After a while, I got used to 'working lunches', but I always knew that as the only woman in the room with clothes on I would never be considered an equal.

Sexism isn't just prevalent in the corporate workplace. When I visit my gynaecologist Dr Lucy, she gives me an account of the medical version.

Dr Lucy is one cool chick. She has a wardrobe to die for and a fantastically relaxed manner. Sometimes when I see her I feel like I'm confiding in one of my friends rather than consulting a medical expert.

I decide to make an appointment to see her – not only because I am about two years overdue for my yearly check-up but because I want to ask her if there is some medical reason for feeling 30-something and over it. I am clinging to the hope that there is a biological explanation for my crisis. If it is a medical problem, then potentially there will be a medical solution. And given that Emma and I started our crisis at the same time, and we are only two months apart in age, maybe our bodies have started producing a new chemical or something – one that can be repressed by a special diet or a couple of pills. Dr Lucy crushes this theory with a raise of an eyebrow and a stifled laugh.

As usual, Dr Lucy looks like a fashion model as I walk into her office, her funky green dress setting off her long red hair trailing down her back. The wall behind her desk is covered with baby cards. I stop counting when I get to 20 cards and feel a tear creep into my eye – not because I've caught the clucky disease but because each card represents a baby, a human life, that she has helped bring into the world. What could possibly be more meaningful than that? When it comes to fulfilling work, surely Lucy has found the ultimate?

Lucy loves her job and always has. She just hates all the bullshit that she had to endure to get to where she is. Her specialisation, obstetrics and gynaecology, is dominated by men. She says she had to fight so hard to get accepted into a training programme and then had to battle every step of the way. In the early days, she was told by the male gatekeepers of the profession that she should give it up now because she'd never make it. It was exhausting, and if she weren't so determined and strong-willed she would have given up. I'm glad she didn't.

Lucy thinks this is the main reason women have lost their give-a-shit. It's just too hard to keep fighting against male structures, conventions and prejudices. For a lot of women, it's just not worth it.

I've just spent the last couple of chapters dumping on men and enlisted the firepower of some of the best female writers of our time and even my gynaecologist to help me out. But it is unfair to point the finger solely at men for women's discontent in the workplace – especially when we girls can be our own worst enemies. Some of my best male friends are bigger feminists than I am, and they already carry around enough white-man's guilt without me adding to it.

I'm constantly shocked and dismayed by the number of passive-aggressive or outright bitchy women I come across at work. I put this down to the fact that they had to fight so hard to get where they are they don't know how to stop being aggressive and defensive. Sometimes I want to shake them and yell, 'We're all on the same team here!'

There's also the destructive gossip we use to sabotage each other. Emma used to work with a woman who was the worst of the worst.

She would spread personal information about people in her team to the rest of the organisation to imply personal weakness. When a woman applied for a job in Emma's team, gossip-girl came to Emma to tell her that the applicant wasn't experienced enough for the job. When Emma ignored her advice, she spread a rumour that the woman was a reformed prostitute.

If the sisterhood had the unity and loyalty of the gay movement, I think we'd all be a lot better off. We'd have a much better chance of abolishing the discrimination, poor conditions for working mothers and networking on the golf course if we banded together rather than fighting amongst ourselves. Why don't women realise that when we undermine each other we are hurting ourselves, because the group that benefits from our actions is men. It's hard to blame men for having all the power when we give them even more of it through our own dysfunctional behaviour. Not to mention that if we were all a little nicer to each other it would be a lot more fun showing up to work each day.

Every woman knows that one of the biggest and most reliable sources of support, comfort and happiness in our lives is our female friends. How tragic and stupid that we have so much trouble replicating this kindness and solidarity in the workplace.

15

BORN-AGAIN IDEALISTS

When I first met Julie she scowled at me. She is ten years older than I am and one rank more senior in our consulting organisation. I had long ago written her off as another one of those passive-aggressive women in the workforce who have abandoned the sisterhood. Under normal circumstances I would have just deleted the email that has been sent out announcing her resignation, but I am intrigued when I read that she is leaving to pursue 'lateral career opportunities'. What does that mean?

It turns out Julie is leaving consulting to join a chemical engineering company that is primarily focused on cleaning up environmental messes. It is also owned by her partner. She met her partner when she was sailing on her own around the South Pacific. Ever since they met, her partner had been trying to recruit her to join his company, but she continually refused because she didn't want to sleep with the boss. Finally, she has capitulated.

The main driver for her career shift is simply that she hasn't been having enough fun. She's been working ridiculous hours, hasn't been well supported by the organisation and wants to do something more enjoyable. 'My time is precious, and I wasn't using it wisely in my current work,' Julie says.

She was frustrated that she had little influence over the work she did. 'My set of values and how I wanted to make a contribution were not consistent with the organisation,' she says. 'The people of influence were too commercially focused and not interested in delivering benefits and value to the client.' Consequently she didn't respect those leaders.

The long hours, stress and lack of support in her job were undermining her self-worth and her health. She was losing weight and couldn't sleep or eat. She was prone to bursting into tears whenever somebody said something nice, and snapping at everybody else. She'd resorted to taking sleeping and anti-anxiety pills, and her self-confidence had plummeted.

'I knew that it was work making me sick, because everything else in my life was going well,' she says.

Then a friend of hers died unexpectedly from a heart attack. 'He was the same age as me,' she says. 'I was standing at the grave site and realised that I didn't want to spend a day longer doing a job I didn't enjoy.' Julie resigned the next day.

She says that now she smiles instead of scowls, and people tell her that she's like a different person. Julie is focused on pleasing herself by doing what is right for her rather than what is right for her employer or her career progression. 'Now I'm doing what is important in my *life* rather than what's important in my *work*,' she says.

If she had her career over again, Julie wouldn't work so hard. She never again wants to do a job that doesn't interest her. She will only work for organisations that have great leaders, a team she can learn from but also help to influence, and values that are aligned to her own.

At the end of the conversation, she thanks me for giving her the opportunity to think about and express her feelings about work and her career. I feel bad that I'd judged her based on our first meeting and didn't consider that her scowl wasn't about me; instead she was just exhausted and deeply unhappy with how she was spending the most part of every day. Perhaps I could have made it a little more bearable for her if I'd shown a little more understanding and support.

What I see in Julie is a return to idealism. She wants to work for an organisation she believes in, in terms of the work they do and the people she works with.

I am also becoming more idealistic, and, until I realised that other people feel the same way, I'd been too embarrassed to admit it. In my youth, I was painfully idealistic, moralistic and even more judgemental than I am now. I was going to save the world and I was going to be a real pain in the arse about it too. I desperately want something to care about and believe in again – something I can spend my time thinking about and working towards. I need a cause, a project, a mission, something that is bigger than myself. I need Godfrey's metaphorical baby.

It seems that there is a plethora of 30-somethings, including me, who have come full circle: started off as idealistic teenagers, got lost in their 20s as they tried to make something of themselves, and now are returning to ideals and meaning when they hit their 30s.

My friend Sara, the lawyer-cum-stay-at-home-mother, studied at Harvard with many ex-investment bankers, ex-consultants and ex-accountants who had returned to study as a way of shifting to a more fulfilling career. Some of them planned to work for NGOs when they finished their studies and others were hoping to apply their corporate skills in the developing world. Another friend recently quit her job at a consulting company to work for an international aid organisation. She was tired of enriching her wallet at the expense of her soul.

Rachel is also a born-again idealist. We used to work together before she went on maternity leave, so I am surprised to hear that the über-ambitious career woman has been transformed. 'I'm not a corporate person any more,' she says. 'I don't want to wear a suit and come into the city every day.'

She admits that she's not the stay-at-home-mum type either. 'I have to do something,' she says. 'The routine of motherhood is dead boring. I need something else to add to my role of mother. But if I'm away from my child, then I should be doing something worthwhile.

If I'm not spending my time enriching his life, then I should be enriching somebody else's.'

Rachel no longer cares about how much money she earns or the power or prestige associated with her job. 'I don't want to do the hours any more,' she says. 'I want to use my brain and I want to make a difference. I want to be part of the community.'

Before having a baby, Rachel was not a community-minded person. Now that she's become a mother and is more involved in the community, she has realised its value. Even though she has returned to consulting on a part-time basis she would prefer to be doing a job where she can give back to the community. She claims that other mothers feel the same.

'There is a huge network of women out there who are so skilled and all want to do something that matters,' she says. 'If you could somehow get that network together, you could do some amazing things. I just don't know how to do it. And these women *do* things. You give a job to a mother, it gets done.'

I ask her if she is happier now that she's a mother. 'I'm richer,' she says. 'I have more dimensions to my life, and life is more meaningful. I've worked out the meaning of life. It's about legacy. The most important thing I can do is leave a really good legacy by raising my son the best that I can.'

16

LIVING THE DREAM

I am looking for a Trustafarian – somebody with a trust fund who doesn't have to work – to validate my theory that the antidote to being 30-something and over it is not as simple as just giving up work. I can't find a Trustafarian – I don't tend to move in old-money circles. But I do find Peter.

Peter started his career as an electrical engineer but jumped aboard the Internet wave just as it was gathering pace. He rode the wave for several years and got off before it crashed, taking his money with him. Now Peter has enough money that he doesn't need to work.

Peter spends his days learning to surf, gliding and getting his pilot's licence. Each new hobby entertains him for a few weeks, and then he becomes bored with it.

Here is a man without constraints on his life. Armed with time, money, youth and health, he can do whatever he wants. From a distance, it seems too good to be true. I have wasted days, maybe even weeks, of my life fantasising about this situation. If only I had enough money not to work, then I'd be happy. Haven't we all dreamt about hitting the jackpot and winning our freedom?

But Peter is anything but free. He is shackled by his abundant options. He is frustrated, unhappy and angry. 'I'm in a bubble, and I don't know how to get out of it,' he says. 'I can do anything I want, but I don't know what to do.'

I ask him what is wrong with what he is doing now – why can't he just keep on mastering new sports and having fun? Once he's mastered surfing and flying, he could entertain himself with other sports or even dabble in artistic pursuits. Surely there are thousands of fun things he could do? But Peter is looking for more than just fun and freedom; like the rest of us, he is seeking purpose and meaning. 'Learning to surf and fly is challenging, but it doesn't give me any sense of being valued and needed,' he says.

'I need to know I'm doing something important. When I was working, I got feedback from my boss and my team that I was doing a good job. It was good for my confidence.'

Peter has considered buying an old house and renovating it. 'It would be nice to do something with my hands, but I know it will be just like surfing – fun for a while, and then I'll be over it.'

So why doesn't he just get another job where he can manage a team and get feedback and validation? He is over that too. It seems Peter got more satisfaction out of working when he needed to work. Now that he doesn't need to work it is hard for him to motivate himself to do it. What a paradox. Peter enjoyed working when he was forced to do it. Now that he can choose not to work, he doesn't get any satisfaction from it. It seems that the very thing I have been striving for – freedom from work – is the very thing that is making Peter miserable.

I compare Peter's predicament with my friend Jamie – the one who doesn't love his job but accepts that he has to work to provide for his family so makes the most of it while he is there. Jamie has a purpose for what he does each day – to provide for his family. That means he doesn't need to get innate enjoyment out of every single task at work because the bigger purpose – his family – is what makes working worthwhile.

Going to work each day to support his beautiful family is noble and meaningful. It is hard to think of a better reason than that to get out of bed. Peter's financial freedom means that he doesn't really have a reason to get out of bed any day – other than perhaps missing his flying lesson. Talking to Peter makes me realise that fun and freedom do not equal fulfilment.

I suggest that perhaps he needs to find a purpose greater than himself and more enduring than the instant pleasures of sports and activities – he needs a baby. He needs something to care about.

Peter agrees with me, but this highlights his biggest problem – he has no idea what his baby can be. He doesn't even know where to start looking for it. To complicate matters, Peter isn't prepared to make any compromises; he isn't going to settle for anything other than total fulfilment. 'I only want the best option,' he says.

It seems to me that Peter is waiting for his 'calling' – an epiphany where he discovers his reason for being, the way some people are born to be mothers or members of the clergy, or like my brother Michael, who knew for sure he was born to be a musician. How wonderful it would be to have such clarity, but from what I can tell, most of us aren't so lucky.

I see a man before me who could possibly spend his whole life searching for his perfect baby, distracting himself from his unhappiness and emptiness with hobbies and fads while life passes him by. 'Maybe it doesn't matter what your baby is,' I suggest. 'Maybe the process of nurturing and developing something is more important than the actual thing you're focusing on. Why don't you just pick something and give it a go?' Peter tells me that he's feeling so frustrated and angry he isn't motivated to do anything at all at the moment.

If I had been in any doubt, talking to Peter has convinced me that working is essential to my well-being and to his. Countless happiness studies suggest that people who work have greater well-being than those who don't. But having said that, it's obvious to me that boring and meaningless work is not good for my well-being either. French writer Albert Camus sums it up beautifully with his quote: 'Without work, all life goes rotten. But when work is soulless, life stifles and dies.' I realise that my journey of discovery is no longer about the merits of working versus not working; it is all about finding the right type of work (and I include parenting in my definition of work). Out of all the people I've spoken to so far I worry about Peter the most. How fascinating, because from the outside looking in you'd think Peter has it made. He is living the dream, but it is a nightmare.

17

DISPENSABLE, IRRELEVANT AND LIBERATED

Sometimes I get paid to do nothing, and I hate it.

In consulting, there is a concept called 'the bench'. It's the closest thing I've experienced to Peter's situation. The bench is a bit like being on the bench at a football match – you're still on the team, but you're not needed at the moment. When you don't have a client, you are considered to be on the bench. You still get paid, but basically you are just waiting until an assignment comes up. What you do when you're on the bench varies depending on the consulting company. Some people have to go to work each day and spend most of the time surfing the Internet, while in other companies they are not required to go into the office at all.

You might think that being on the bench sounds fantastic. I thought it was too good to be true when I first started consulting, and I was right. The bench is the pits. It's great for a week while you catch up on your personal administration and get a haircut, but after that it becomes soul destroying. It's not like a holiday, because you can't escape from the nagging feeling that you should be working and contributing. Damn that work ethic.

And because you're not contributing to anything, you don't get any feedback or validation. In short, you don't feel needed. But the worst thing about it for me is that it's lonely. So much of the dialogue I engage in each day is work-related. When I'm not working on a project, I don't have anybody to talk to, other than brief snippets at the water cooler.

My experience on the bench reinforces my realisation that I'm not 'over' doing something. I still want to achieve, and I still want to feel like I'm contributing. I can also say that I'm still ambitious. I'm just ambitious for something else. I want to contribute and succeed at something that is meaningful to me. Many of the people I've spoken to agree. They either know of a worthwhile project they would do instead of their current job, if they could afford it, or they are trying to find one. It seems very few of us don't want to work – we just don't want to do meaningless, unsatisfying or stressful work.

In *I Could Do Anything If I Only Knew What It Was*, Barbara Sher says that finding a sense of meaning is essential to our happiness, not just in work but also in play. She believes we will never be happy just amusing ourselves and advises against choosing a permanent vacation as a life goal, even in retirement. Interestingly, out of all the people I've spoken to who hate their jobs, very few of them dream of a life of leisure as the alternative. So don't get me wrong, I'm not advocating idleness. When I first realised I was over it, I worried that I was just lazy. But I'm pretty sure that that's not it. The idea of planning my life around watching daytime soap operas is horrifying.

Barbara Sher says that in order to find meaningful work we need to understand the connection between doing what we love and doing something worth doing – something that has meaning.

I was raised to believe that to do something meaningful or worthwhile it had to be for the good of others and most likely would require a personal sacrifice. Like most little girls, I grew up believing that doing something just for yourself was just plain selfish. And of course, the very worst thing in the world to be is selfish, particularly if you're a woman. Being selfish is even worse than dealing drugs to preschoolers or mixing your colours in the washing machine.

Fuck that. Barbara Sher agrees with me. She says that Picasso and Einstein weren't necessarily trying to help anybody in their work; they were just doing something that they loved and that was important to them. Their motivation was personal and self-absorbed, yet the by-product was an enormous contribution to the world. 'It's not about choosing between doing something for yourself or something for others, but rather they are one and the same – to do one you must do the other,' she says.

I suppose that's what Julie, the consultant who resigned to do environmental work, is doing by joining the chemical engineering company – she's pleasing herself by doing work she enjoys, and she's cleaning up the environment as well. Both Chris and my brother Michael are pleasing themselves by writing for a living – one with words, the other with music – and yet they are both gifting the world with beauty and insight.

But having said that, we aren't all lucky enough to fall in love in the South Pacific with a chemical engineer on an environmental mission like Julie. Nor can we all be artists like Michael and Chris. Not everybody has the talent, the inclination or the luxury to live this way. Despite what the career-guidance books say, the realist in me says that a good proportion of us have no other option than to do laborious, repetitive, meaningless work in order to survive.

Nigel Marsh will tell you that laborious, repetitive work does not have to be meaningless. In *Fat, Forty and Fired*, he wrote that his main role as CEO of an advertising agency was to create a sense of meaning for his employees.

Really? In my mind, the main role of a CEO is to suck up to the board and appease the shareholders. I find his claim very noble but highly unbelievable, so I ask him to explain.

'Many CEOs lead with a message of fear,' Marsh says. 'They say to their staff, "You have to pay rent, so you need this job, so I'm going to make you work really, really hard to make me a little bit richer." It's soul destroying.'

Marsh says that work need not be that way. 'A good leader can construct and communicate meaning in employees' working lives. Meaning can be created by a shared endeavour or a common goal. It could come from wanting to beat the competition, be the first, do something differently or uphold a tradition.'

He gives me an example of working for a bus company. 'Rather than telling people that this is the only bus company in the city they can work for so they should just keep their noses clean and get on with it, a good leader can help the employees see how valuable their jobs are – providing transportation for a city.'

Apparently JFK also shared Marsh's view of leadership. Leading with meaning is considered to be one of the reasons why the NASA Space Programme in the 1960s was so successful. The more cynical explanation for the enormous achievement has something to do with a Disney movie studio. The story goes that JFK had done such a good job of creating a shared purpose that on one occasion when he was touring NASA a janitor replied in response to a query about what he was doing there: 'Putting the first man on the moon, sir.' Putting the first man on the moon was a far more meaningful occupation to the janitor than showing up each day to pick up rubbish.

I'd like to think that this leadership strategy is more than just a way of manipulating employees with rhetoric. And Marsh does caution that it is essential that leaders actually believe it themselves. He says, 'We can't all be Mother Teresa and change the world, but imagine what a difference it would make if all our leaders had a slightly nobler purpose.'

It's a nice thought, but I'm not sure it's enough to turn an unsatisfying job into a satisfying one.

Another thing that must affect the sense of meaning we get from work is the realisation that we are dispensable. This is a radical change from my ambitious 20-something days to my discontented 30-something days. I used to believe I was indispensable – that the work I did was so important and the knowledge that I had acquired was so unique that the project simply couldn't function without me. Bitter experience has proved me wrong.

I've seen enough people come and go from organisations to know that it actually doesn't matter whose bum is in the chair – things just keep rolling on. Or not.

Emma says that when she was younger she thought that she was important to the organisation that she worked for and that she should be listened to. Now she knows that organisations don't give a crap about her or anybody else. 'And why should they?' she says. 'Companies don't care about people; they only care about commerce. If we make them money, then they are happy. If not, then you're out.'

Emma's attitude changed when her previous company reorganised and retrenched a whole lot of people. Some of them had given a lot to the business, but when things changed and they weren't needed any more they were out. 'Once you've seen people be retrenched you realise that work is not about fulfilling people's lives or making them better people. It will never be about individuals when there are 50 zillion other people out there. Once you understand that, you're over it. You lose your give-a-shit when you realise *they* don't give a shit.'

I meet a guy at a party who works in medical research and who feels just as insignificant as Emma and I do. He is working on immunisation and disease prevention. I say, 'Wow, that must be satisfying work.' He replies, 'No. Not really. There are so many people all over the world working on the same thing, it doesn't matter what I do.' He says knowing that if he doesn't do the research, somebody else will, or probably already is, makes him wonder why he bothers.

Oliver James in *Affluenza* talks about employees being reduced to commodities that are bought by organisations and easily substituted for another. 'Just how much this way of thinking is taken for granted is shown by the name given to . . . Human Resources [Departments]. It used to be called Personnel. The new name indicates how the humans who work for the company are indistinguishable from the computers or widgets or financial services that the company buys and sells.'

In an odd way, the realisation that I am dispensable and essentially irrelevant is liberating. It means that I don't *have* to do anything. I realise that my source of meaning can be, and has to be, personal. I can free myself from any parental or social expectation about what I *should* do, because the world doesn't need *me* to do it. Just like the medical researcher at the party, there are plenty of other people to do whatever it is I am expected to do.

In the manner of selfish Einstein or selfish Picasso, this realisation frees me to search for something that is important to *me*.

18

NOT ENOUGH

Sonia once had a meaningful job. She made a difference to children's lives, yet on Sunday nights she would cry at the thought of going to work on Monday.

Sonia was a teacher for 11 years. She loved teaching and had ambitions of becoming a deputy principal. She had great mentors and worked with colleagues who shared her values and vision: people who taught for the love of it and had the best interests of the kids at heart.

The low social status and value accorded to teachers didn't bother Sonia because she felt valued by her students. 'If every year I made a real difference in one kid's personal life, then it was worth doing,' she says. 'I still have kids visit me years after they have left school. The relationship continues, so I know that my impact was more than just in the classroom.'

I am confused. It sounds to me like Sonia is describing the ultimate – a job that is meaningful, that she enjoyed, with a career path, and colleagues she liked and respected. How could she have ticks in all those boxes and still have the Sunday Night Blues?

Sonia was physically and emotionally exhausted. 'Teaching is stressful and draining,' she said. 'It doesn't matter if you have good kids or bad kids. Kids are not the drain. The drain is that as a teacher you are constantly "on". Some days I didn't even have time to go to the toilet. And then I would take home corrections to do every night. If I didn't do the corrections they haunted me. I'd feel guilty for not doing them.'

If it wasn't corrections, Sonia's evenings, weekends and holidays were filled with report writing, administration and preparation. On top of that, she had to deal with unrealistic demands from parents. On a couple of occasions, she was even physically threatened by parents. Even though she felt supported by the school, it was still traumatic. 'If the job were just in the classroom and just teaching kids, I would have done it until I was 60,' Sonia says.

When she met her husband, she realised that she didn't want to come home from work every day feeling so tired and drained. 'I couldn't do anything during the week because I was so tired.' She wanted to be able to do things with her husband, but she didn't have the time or the emotional energy.

Her job even got in the way of her marriage proposal. Sonia's husband booked a holiday to propose to her but had to change the flights and accommodation bookings because she had reports to write.

Sonia tried to solve the problem by changing schools. She moved from a big school in the city to a smaller school in the country hoping that she would be less stressed and more invigorated. She wasn't. Sonia could see herself getting trapped in a downward spiral of unhappiness. She started putting on weight, which made her even more unhappy and tired. 'I realised that down the track my relationship would pay the price, too,' she says.

I ask Sonia why she didn't slow down a bit and take the pressure off herself. If she didn't want to do corrections each night, surely she didn't have to? If she didn't want to spend her weekends and holidays preparing for classes, then why do it?

But it is obvious that Sonia is not the sort of person who could just clock on and clock off as a teacher. She cared deeply about her students, so as well as taking home corrections every night, I suspect she was also taking home the stress and emotional worries. She tells me about one of her students who committed suicide. 'He came to my office to see me, but I wasn't there,' she says. 'A few weeks later, he killed himself. His mother came up and spoke to me at the funeral. She remembered me from the parent–teacher interviews. She spoke to me for about 20 minutes, saying that her son always talked about me, and then she invited me back to the house for the wake. I was the only person invited who wasn't family.'

Sonia's eyes well with tears and so do mine. My tears are for the poor boy who felt like he had no options, and for my mother who had clearly felt the same when she tried to hang herself in my flat. But mostly my tears are for Sonia. We will never know if the boy would still be with us today if Sonia had been in her office when he came to see her, and even though it is irrational for Sonia to shoulder such responsibility, it is so moving to see how much she cares.

'I wish I could have pulled back,' she says. 'But when I teach I'm totally involved, and I can't teach any other way. I can't give less than 100 per cent. The only thing I could do was leave.'

Sonia started investigating other career options, such as opening a bed and breakfast hotel or a chocolate shop. When a friend suggested she open a bookstore, she decided to try it out and found a part-time job in a local bookshop to learn about the industry and see if she enjoyed it. She worked weekends in the bookshop and taught during the week until she had enough confidence to take the plunge and open her own bookstore.

Sonia's bookshop is more than just a place that sells books. It's an educational environment. She uses her teaching skills in running the store by writing newsletters and running workshops for customers. Each month, she holds a workshop for parents about childhood literacy.

'Only 57 per cent of parents read to their children daily. I want to have a hand in fixing that,' she says. 'I still feel like I'm making a difference. I have over 1,200 loyal customers, and through the book clubs and workshops I feel like I'm doing the same thing as when I was teaching.'

Since leaving teaching and opening the bookstore, Sonia is happier and healthier. 'My husband says I am so much calmer and relaxed, and I'm able to switch off at night,' she says.

'I come home a lot happier, because I don't think about the store when I leave it. Three days a month, I have to work at night to do the books and administration, but other than that I have my nights and weekends back. I've got my time and energy back during the week.'

There is still some stress in Sonia's life. The main stress is financial. 'We've essentially gone back to one income,' she says. 'I feel bad that I'm costing the relationship an income, but my husband is happy that I'm happy.'

The bookshop is breaking even at the moment, but Sonia is realistic enough to know that if it doesn't make money eventually she'll have to shut it down. 'I'm going to give it two years, and if I can't make it into a profitable business then we'll have to cut our losses and move on to the next thing. I don't need to make a lot of money. If I can draw the same wage from the store as I did teaching, then I'll be happy.'

Sonia acknowledges that she could only open the store because her circumstances allowed it. 'We could afford it because we don't have kids,' she says. 'I'm lucky enough to have a husband who is willing and able to support me while I take this risk.'

As I drive home from Sonia's bookshop, I start to cry again. What have I ever done in my career to touch people's lives the way Sonia has? When have I made a difference to anything other than an organisation's bottom line?

I am determined to find something meaningful to do with my time. Although, after speaking to Sonia I now realise that meaning is not enough. Sonia had a meaningful job, yet she worked so hard and cared so much it almost destroyed her. She needed balance as well as meaning.

19

WAKE-UP CALL

Emma phones when I am on my way to my second interview at ABC Company. I am focused on the interview, so I let her call go through to my voicemail.

The interview goes well. I am grilled for almost two hours on change management theory and practice by a very clever, very experienced and slightly eccentric consultant. I enjoy the intellectual sparring, think I've held my own and leave feeling confident.

I pick up Emma's message as I am leaving the office. Her message just says to call her back, but my blood runs cold at the tone of her voice. It is the first time I've ever heard Emma sound scared. She is without doubt the most well-balanced, resilient person I know. At the worst moments of her life, she is always calm and philosophical. I know something must be seriously wrong.

Emma and I went to the same high school. Although we are the same age, she was one year above me at school. All through high school, I was scared of her. She was one of the cool kids who hung around with the pretty girls, and I was a nerd. While she was smoking behind the shed, I was in the library with the debating team. But by the time we went to university, I realised we were not so different – she'd just been to more nightclubs before we were legally allowed to drink than I had.

When Emma left school, she spent one year studying education. She thought she wanted to be a teacher until she had her first taste of classroom experience and discovered she didn't like children. The following year, she transferred onto the same communications course that I was doing. And this was when we formed the bond of friendship that has endured ever since.

When my family fell apart, Emma was there. When my relationships turned sour, Emma was there. When I was so depressed I didn't care if I lived or died, Emma was there. She taught me about sisterhood, eyelash curlers and spray tans, convinced me to buy Toffee my dog and introduced me to erotic literature and vibrators.

I'm not prepared when she says, 'I might have cervical cancer.'

Emma went to the doctor for a general check-up because she was continuing to lose weight and had had the flu for over two months straight. The doctor took blood and urine and gave her a smear test. The smear test found that she had advanced pre-cancer cells on her cervix. Smear test results are notoriously inaccurate, so the doctor warned her that potentially some of the cells could be cancerous as well. He sent her to see Dr Lucy the funky gynaecologist for further tests.

Cervical cancer is the second most common cancer that affects women. The main cause is the human papillomavirus (HPV). If your body can't fight the infection, abnormal cells can develop in the lining of your cervix. These abnormal cells can then become cervical pre-cancer and then cancer. In most cases, this process can take years, although in Emma's case it has only taken a few months. She'd had a smear test only 12 months earlier that came back normal. But now her pre-cancer cells are considered advanced, which means if she doesn't have cancerous cells already she could get them any day.

Dr Lucy's tests come back with the same results: advanced pre-cancer cells on the cervix. Emma needs to have a biopsy of the cervix to get a more accurate diagnosis.

Waiting for the surgery is excruciating. It is only two weeks but it feels like two years. After the initial shock from the smear test results, Emma has slipped back into her standard philosophical mode, insisting that worrying is futile. I, on the other hand, am not so calm. Every time I speak to her, I imagine the greedy little cells eating her up from the inside out until there is nothing left of her.

It turns out Emma was right – worrying was futile and unnecessary. The biopsy reveals that none of the cells have turned cancerous yet, nor have they spread outside her cervix. Dr Lucy removed all the nasty little bastards during the biopsy.

So how did Emma catch HPV? The most common cause is unprotected sex. It's possible she contracted it from riding bare-back with all-brawn-no-brains-stamina-boy. Alternatively, the virus could have been lying dormant in her body for years and only took hold after her non-stop partying when her immune system simply couldn't cope any more. Who would have thought that the price of Emma's thrisis would be so high?

Nonetheless, Emma is exceptionally lucky. Relatively speaking, a biopsy and a couple of weeks of worry is getting off easily. If the HPV hadn't been diagnosed in time, she could have ended up needing a hysterectomy and chemotherapy. Instead, she escapes with a massive fright and the conviction that she needs to clean up her life.

Dr Lucy warns Emma that she needs to stay healthy to boost her immune system to make sure the virus doesn't return. She sends Emma to a doctor who specialises in post-operative health and chronic fatigue. He says Emma is a classic post-viral case – her immune system has broken down and needs to be rebuilt. She is prescribed basic nutrition, regular sleep, gentle exercise and vitamin injections.

Like most of us, Emma thought she was invincible. 'Of course I understood the cause-and-effect relationship between how I treat my body and how I feel,' she says. 'I just didn't think it applied to me. And because the effects aren't immediate I just got into a pattern of abusing my body.'

It takes Emma over six months to regain her health. She is tired, run-down and pale. But copious amounts of sleep and vegetable juice do the trick.

Once Emma starts feeling better, we decide to deal with our 30-something and over it crisis a little more conservatively – self-help books.

20

SELF-HELP

There are so many books about defining your career path, finding your passion and discovering your strengths and skills. It begs the question, when there are so many books in the world to assist us in finding career satisfaction, why are so many of us discontented and miserable?

You can't help but question their effectiveness, but the truth is I'm a sucker for a self-help book. I wish I weren't. I wish I could tell you that I was above it, but I'd be lying. Not only do I love the idea of continually improving myself, I also really enjoy reading them. I can't help it; I've always been a nerd.

I'm not alone. I meet Amanda at a party. She is a university lecturer in IT and her 30-something crisis seems to have been going for about ten years. She turned to self-help books to discover her life purpose and is working part-time so she can spend the rest of the time searching for answers.

She's read them all – from the classics like *What Should I Do With My Life?* and *What Color Is Your Parachute?*, to the New Age books such as the *Celestine Prophecy* and *The Power of Now*.

One of Amanda's favourites is *Do What You Are* by Paul D. Tieger and Barbara Barron. The basis of this book is that you have to do a job that suits your personality type – one that matches your values and definition of success. The book is based on the 16 Myers-Briggs personality types and claims to help you discover your personality type and then lists professions and job characteristics that suit or don't suit your type. Amanda learned that she's a highly sensitive person, and people with her personality type can't just settle for a job simply because it pays the bills. She wishes she could just do a job for money and then do fulfilling things at home, but she needs more than that.

I leave the party early to go home and do the exercise in *Do What You Are*, and I discover that my personality type is ENTP – Extroverted, Intuitive, Thinking and Perceiving. People like me have good communication skills, are motivated by being around people, are entrepreneurial and have creative problem-solving skills. On the downside, I am also disorganised, prone to exaggeration, get bored easily and am intolerant of people whose competence I question and people who are unimaginative and inflexible. After summing up my personality so accurately, I eagerly flip over to the page that lists my ideal profession. My ideal profession is . . . wait for it . . . a management consultant. Other suggestions include a journalist and an employee relations specialist.

If you categorise all the jobs I've had in my career, you would come up with just that – a management consultant, a journalist and an employee relations specialist. It's nice to know I've chosen professions that suit my personality type. And I even did it without the help of Paul D. Tieger and Barbara Barron. Paul and Barbara get full marks for matching my personality type with jobs that I'm good at. Unfortunately, I'm no closer to discovering the formula for job satisfaction.

The one thing I do take away from *Do What You Are* is the realisation that I need to be around people to be motivated and energised. Being an extrovert, I know that I'm unlikely to be happy sitting in an office with the door closed, bashing away on a computer every day. I need to be out and about mixing with people, bouncing ideas off others and getting energised by interactions.

Other than the fact that I can't afford the lifestyle, knowing that

I'm an extrovert is a big reason why my friend Godfrey's advice that I should become a writer doesn't feel right to me. I love writing, but I worry that if I make it my profession rather than just a hobby I will end up hating it. There are not too many things in my life that I can honestly say I love doing. It would be stupid to risk screwing up my love of writing by making it more significant in my life than it should be.

I ring Emma with the bad news. I tell her that I can't become a writer because I'm an ENTP. She says, 'You think that's bad. I'm an ESTJ – that is the same personality type as Hitler. I'm narcissistic, arrogant, dominating and aggressive.' I flick over to the section in the book that lists the ideal careers for Emma and Hitler. Some of the suggested career options are: military officer, funeral director and a regulatory compliance officer. 'These are jobs from hell,' Emma says. 'As if I would ever do any of them.'

After the less-than-enlightening results from doing the exercises in *Do What You Are*, I struggle to complete the discovery exercises in all the other self-help books I read. I just can't motivate myself to get out the crayons and draw pictures encompassing everything my parents, siblings, teachers, neighbours and pets wanted me to do with my life. Nor can I be arsed filling up a notebook with all the things that make me angry, scared or hurt. Why can't I just skip the exercises and go straight to the chapter that has the answers? Upon reflection, it's possible that I've missed the point.

Emma doesn't have much luck with the self-help books either. She diligently completes every exercise in Barbara Sher's *I Could Do Anything If I Only Knew What It Was*, and, even though she gets a better understanding of what has influenced her career choices, she doesn't have any revelations about what she should do with her life. 'I got lots of clarity about the influence of my parents' expectations on my life choices,' she says. 'And I have a better understanding of the types of things I'm good at, but it didn't link to anything. I was expecting to get to the end of the exercises and the answer would leap off the page: like I should be a fireman or something.'

I ask Amanda what she's learned from all the books. She says the most important thing is that you can't sit around all day contemplating. The most effective strategy is to do things, try things. I don't need to point out the irony of her spending the last six months doing nothing other than reading books. She says the books provide her with answers, but then when she gets back into ordinary life it all just disappears. 'It's nice and it's intellectual,' she says. 'But it hasn't sunk in.'

But Amanda is enjoying working part-time. She likes that on her days off she's not expected to do anything for anybody other than herself. 'Now I have time to enjoy breakfast by the river,' she says.

I marvel at Amanda's patience. If I'd spent the best part of a year reading self-help books and hadn't changed a single thing in my life, or wasn't any happier or fulfilled, I'd feel cheated and pissed off. Being 30-something and over it is no picnic – I want to sort this mess out as soon as possible. Waking up each morning not knowing my purpose is confronting and it's scary. It's also isolating.

One of the things I fear most on my 30-something and over it journey is losing my friends. I worry that if I don't give a shit about work any more, I also won't give a shit about a good deal of what my friends talk about.

I haven't realised before now how much time I spend talking about work with my friends. We talk about the stupid things our managers and clients do, our levels or ranks within our organisations, our career paths and promotions, and our bonuses. Without my give-a-shit, I don't have much to contribute. If I don't have work in common with my friends any more, then maybe there won't be enough common ground to bind us together.

I am ashamed of myself after I have coffee with my friend Todd. He tells me excitedly that he will soon be promoted from level six to level seven in his organisation. It takes all the discipline I can muster to stifle a yawn and not say what I am thinking – 'Who cares? Levels are just arbitrary social constructs.' I don't want to be like this. I want to be excited for him.

Six months ago, I would have been excited for him – and envious, too. But now I feel like I can't relate to what he is saying. I've changed, and it is terrifying. This isn't the point of my 30-something journey. My journey is supposed to make me more fulfilled and happier. I'm pretty sure that losing my friends and sense of belonging won't help me reach that objective.

Risking my friendships and therefore my sense of belonging on some meaning-and-purpose crusade is nothing more than fucked up. My unspoken response to Todd is arrogant and elitist. And while I feel like I am making some progress in finding my give-a-shit again, I need to remind myself that any path that will not allow me to take my friends with me is surely headed in the wrong direction.

But despite my commitment to maintaining my friendships, the social engagements that used to invigorate me are leaving me cold. Friday-night drinks after work and other networking functions and parties make me feel empty and lonely. The new guy who is ingratiating himself with me because I might advance his career starts to annoy me, and the friend who phones me on the third Tuesday of every month 'just to say hi', whilst nurturing his networking investment, infuriates me. The transactional nature of my relationships with people has become blatantly apparent. It is as if we are all commodities that exist purely for opportunistic reasons: an investment we keep warm in case we can use each other in the future.

It is crushing to realise that most of the people I spend most of my time with are not actually my friends. When I count my real friends – the ones who have endured through different phases of my life, the ones I can call in the middle of the night in despair, the ones who love me just the way I am – they fit on one hand, and I have fingers to spare.

I have confused the concepts of friendship and association, and by doing so I have done my friends a grave disservice. I have been guilty in the past of prioritising networking opportunities over the needs of friends – not having time to see them for months and months because I was too busy building my career. Thank God they stuck by me while I came to my senses. I guess that's what makes them friends.

Emma has never fallen into the 'networking' trap. In fact, she was told by her manager that her unwillingness to network is a weakness. Emma puts her intolerance of networking down to her education at a government school. 'We didn't learn the value of networking when we were at school because there wasn't anybody there worth knowing.' She avoids networking functions now because she can't bear the opportunism. 'Everybody there is just trying to get something out of you. It's not based on enjoying each other's company,' she says. Emma doesn't want relationships based on what she can get out of people. 'And it's a waste of time, anyway,' she says. 'As if you're going to recommend somebody for something on the basis of a two-minute conversation over a cheap glass of champagne in a tacky hotel lobby.'

One of Emma's associates is a consummate networker. Every time Emma sees her she kisses the air on either side of Emma's head and says, 'Hi, darling, let's do lunch.' 'What's the point?' Emma says. 'She's an idiot. I'm not going to suck up her arse just in case I might one day get a job out of her.'

I find that once I untangle my friends and associates in my mind I become more tolerant and appreciative of my acquaintances. I return to the wisdom of Rodney, the consultant with the life-balancing concentric circles, about expectations and happiness. I expected too much from my professional associates. They are not my friends, and I shouldn't expect them to be. While it is fun to socialise with them, and mutually beneficial to network with them, I shouldn't expect them to be anything other than what they are.

Both have a role to play in my life: the important thing is to know how to tell the difference.

21

40-SOMETHING AND INTO IT

When I confess to Caroline that I am 30-something and over it, she says, 'I remember what that feels like. I used to be like that, but now I'm 40-something and into it.'

Caroline is my mentor. I met her when I first started consulting and have kept her as my mentor ever since. I chose her as my mentor because she was a change management consultant the same as I am, and a respected senior woman. Most of all, I clicked with her and I trusted her. Some people advise that the best mentor is somebody completely different from yourself, possibly somebody you don't even like because then you get a completely different perspective on things. This is not the case with Caroline: I like her and admire her.

Over the last few years, Caroline has transitioned from being a full-time consultant and a part-time career and life coach to becoming a full-time coach. It was during this transition that she got over being over it and started being into it.

She loves coaching. It's her passion, and she simply can't do enough, know enough or read enough about it. Sometimes she feels like a fraud because she's getting paid to do something that she loves so much.

It wasn't as simple as just changing careers to transition from being over it to into it. Through the process of learning to be a coach, she underwent some radical adjustments in the way she views herself and the way she lives her life.

Caroline started to get curious about herself and the world around her. 'Curiosity and judgement can't exist in the same space together. It was so liberating to realise I don't have to be judgemental all the time. Now I know how to leave my baggage at the door, and, when I need to, pick it up again.'

Being less judgemental has allowed Caroline to look at what is possible rather than focus on what she should and shouldn't do. This has opened up professional and personal possibilities she wouldn't otherwise have had. Previously all her friends were the same – educated, successful and affluent. Now she has allowed herself to build relationships with people who don't fit the stereotype. 'I had a limited and constrained map of the world,' she says. 'I was limited by my fear and a lack of willingness to challenge my own thinking.'

She now has the self-awareness to detect which of her beliefs empower her and which ones don't work for her any more. Caroline doesn't need to control everything in her life any more, and she no longer needs to have her whole life mapped out for her. 'I missed out on a lot of spontaneous joy in my life because I had to control everything,' she says. 'The more you try to line up all the ducks in your life, the more they'll just shit on you.'

In her 30s, Caroline spent a lot of time comparing what she had with what others had. 'In my 40s, I started asking how I can be kinder to myself. I now ask myself kinder questions.'

Caroline specialises in coaching people who are looking for a sea change. 'Most clients have a romantic view that a simpler life will bring them happiness. But most of the time it's not what they end up doing. Through coaching, they often find another way to give them the satisfaction they are seeking.'

I ask her how coaching can help somebody who is 30-something and over it, and she says it depends on the person. Primarily people need a compelling reason to change: they need to get to the point where they are over being over it. An awareness or even mild discontent is not enough. 'It is not until something has become intolerable that we are forced into action,' she says.

'Some people enjoy being martyrs or thrive on the attention they get as a result of being unhappy. Being dissatisfied works for them: they revel in being victims. Some people need to be stuck for a while before they are prepared to do whatever it takes to move on.

'If people are ready for coaching, then coaching will help them recognise where they are now – confronting the brutal facts of their reality. It will then help them identify where they want to be and give them strategies to get there. Mostly this involves getting clarity about your values and working out which beliefs are not serving you and replacing them with ones that empower you now and in the future.'

'That sounds great,' I say. 'But what happens when you simply don't know where you want to be and what you want to do?' I tell her about all the people I've spoken to who have read every self-help book and even done the exercises in the books and still don't have the answers.

'How many books have you read that have actually changed your behaviour?' Caroline asks. 'A book won't show you when you're sabotaging yourself. Coaching provides the objectivity, skill and courage to shine the mirror back on you in a completely safe environment. It gives you great questions that you wouldn't otherwise think to ask yourself and then gives you the confidence and other internal resources to propel you into action.'

Caroline believes that being 30-something and over it is a good thing. It means that taking the easy route of passively following our path and meeting everyone else's expectations has become so intolerable that we now have a compelling reason to make positive changes in our lives.

'One of the cures for the 30-something blues is about taking control of your own destiny,' Caroline says. 'Even if you end up doing exactly the same thing as you were doing before, having the courage to think about what you want and then consciously and deliberately choosing it makes all the difference.'

A common theme with Caroline's 30-something clients is that they are trying to reject everything they have now rather than embracing it and working out which bits they can keep and use. 'It's really important to recognise that you don't have to change everything,' she says. 'It's often too big a leap to walk away from what you do well, and it's not helpful for people to end up thinking they've wasted that last ten years of their life.'

She says that rather than running away from what we are good at we need to work out how we can build on it to create something better. Sonia the teacher-cum-bookshop owner has intuitively done what Caroline recommends. She didn't just walk away from her years of experience and the skills she developed while teaching, but instead she harnessed the good things, such as her passion for education and ability to relate to kids, and applied them in a new situation. Sonia told me that once she transferred the same ambition into a different area she felt invigorated instead of drained.

Caroline asks me what parts of my previous experience are useful enough to keep and transfer into something new. I suppose I would like to hold onto my writing skills from the first part of my career and the people management or organisation knowledge from consulting. But I still don't know where or how I should apply them.

Caroline is quick to point out that what will work for me in my 30s is unlikely to work for me in my 40s. 'Isn't it good that it doesn't have to?' she says. 'There is no such thing as "the answer" which will last for life. It's arrogant to think that there is. Everyone needs to work out for themselves what works for them.'

22

GETTING FROM A TO B

Kate has figured out what works for her.

When my cousin introduced me to his fiancée, I thought, 'Wow, he's done well.' Kate is witty, worldly and passionate. She has the guts to argue politics with her father-in-law and the eloquence to pull it off. At their wedding, Kate was described in the speeches as being 'beautiful, inside and out'.

She's also another woman who is 40-something and into it.

It wasn't always that way. In her 30s, she was just as discontented and over it as I am, but then she made some changes in her life and found her give-a-shit again. I wonder how she got from A to B, A being awful and B being bliss.

When Kate was in her late 20s, she was slaving away as an account manager in an insurance broking company. At 29, she was promoted to senior management. Kate felt like she had something to prove: she was the youngest person in the company in such a senior role, and she was female. So she worked long hours, took on lots of responsibility and even more stress, and no longer had time for her family and friends. 'I had such high standards for myself,' she says. 'I lost myself.'

Kate also lost her health. She was diagnosed with an acute immune disorder and still has the scars as a constant reminder of what happens when she burns herself out. Her immune system broke down and she started getting eruptions on her skin among a host of other nasty symptoms.

On doctor's orders, she took two weeks off work to rest. She used the time to reassess what was important in her life and decided to quit her job. She traded the big salary, the company car, the status and the corporate perks to become a full-time student. Kate enrolled in an arts degree and studied history, English and cultural studies for three years.

During that time, she developed an interest in interior design and landed a part-time job in the building industry to try her hand at interior design and earn a bit of cash. 'I was happy then,' she says. 'I was engaged with what I was doing and had lots of freedom.'

At age 33 and with a newly minted university degree, she went back to work full-time at the same insurance broking company. I feel disappointed to hear this. 'I don't understand,' I say. 'After breaking free, how could you go back to do it all again?'

Kate says that giving up corporate life was a bit like giving up smoking. She knew it was bad for her, but it still took her a couple of attempts to find the courage to do it. 'And I naively hoped that somehow the second time would be different because, unlike before, I managed an account that was less stressful, slower paced and had normal hours,' she says.

It was going well for a while. The content of the work wasn't overly exciting, but she was intellectually challenged enough to be satisfied. 'But one day things just started to seem pointless,' Kate says. 'I didn't want to get up every day to do something I wasn't connected to or that I wasn't interested in.'

Kate had become 30-something and over it. Like Emma and me, there wasn't a trigger or a dramatic event that changed the way she viewed her work. It just happened. She started to notice a difference between her values and those of her employer. 'I don't think my values had changed,' she says. 'But all of a sudden I just became more aware of them.'

She particularly started noticing the misalignment of values when it came to environmental and ethical issues. And it started to bother her that she was treated differently from her male colleagues. 'I was tired of being a woman in a conservative male industry,' she says.

Kate wanted to move towards something that would let her expand and discover new ways of being. She also craved autonomy. 'I wanted to be in control of my own destiny rather than depend on something external,' she says.

Around the same time, she agreed to marry my cousin Nathan and started thinking about having children. 'There was no way I would be able to find a balance with having children and working at that organisation.' So Kate resigned from her job and took a month off. In that time, she slept in, read books and decided to turn her interior design hobby into a business.

Four and half years later, Kate is running her own business and going from strength to strength. This is not surprising. She's great at it. I know from personal experience. When I bought my flat, I hired her to renovate my bathroom and kitchen. Then when Chris moved in – along with over a thousand of his favourite books – she managed to design cabinetry to store them without turning the flat into a library. When Kate was measuring up for the cabinets, I asked her if she enjoyed her work. She said, 'I love it so much it doesn't even feel like work. I'm doing what I enjoy, and I'm lucky enough to get paid for it.'

Kate didn't do any planning or preparation before she started her business. She just did it. She said that she was fortunate to be in a strong enough position to maintain her financial independence while the business was growing. 'Even though I was in a relationship, I still wanted to be financially independent.'

On the whole, she is really happy with the decision, but it did have its challenges in the beginning. Moving from being a full-time employee to running her own business took some adjustment. 'I missed not having colleagues to bounce ideas off, and I missed the social aspect,' she says. 'But it's not an issue any more. I'm a lot busier now compared with when I first started, and I've learned to enjoy my time alone. I'm not scared of my own company any more. In fact, now I feel like I need it.'

She also missed the structure. 'I tend to get distracted,' Kate says. 'And losing the financial security of a regular wage also took a bit of getting used to. There are ups and downs, but I've learned to ride the waves.'

Kate is calmer now and a lot less interested in material things. 'Maybe it's because I'm not faced with a materialistic environment every day. I don't have to worry about who has what company car and what shoes I'm wearing.

'I consider myself to be a really fortunate person, so I feel like I need to give something back,' she says. Even though Kate tries to give her clients more environmentally sound and safer options in her designs, she sometimes questions the frivolity of what she does. 'I feel like I need to balance my work with things that are more meaningful,' she says. 'So I do volunteer work, spend more time with my friends and family, and get involved in the community.

'Life isn't perfect, of course,' Kate says. 'And it's not set in stone either. In 12 months' time, I might wander down another track. I'm open to that, and I find it exciting.'

Kate has a similar attitude to her career as Caroline the coach. Both of them are liberated rather than constrained by the belief that what they are doing now doesn't have to be for ever. In a way, they have taken the pressure off themselves, which makes it easier to enjoy their jobs and their lives. It occurs to me that when people ask themselves 'Is this it?' a lot of the time the answer is 'Yes, so just get on with it.' Whereas with Kate and Caroline, the answer is 'Only if I choose it to be.'

Kate doesn't define herself by her job the way she used to. 'I don't feel like I've arrived anywhere or it's the end of the story,' she says. Consequently, she hasn't invested her identity in the success of her business and doesn't seem to have the fear of failure that you might expect. 'If it doesn't work out, I'll just find something else to do,' she says.

Talking to Kate makes me realise that up until now my career has been inseparable from my identity. I would proudly introduce myself at parties and wait for the inevitable question 'What do you do?' so I could let everybody know that I was a career woman. What a prat.

Emma used to be the same. When she was growing up, she felt like the entire focus was on getting a good education and a well-paid job. It was even more important than being a well-rounded person or having a family. 'Our parents wanted the best for us and wanted us to be happy,' Emma says. 'But because of all the pressure to get a good job, we assumed that the best way to achieve happiness was through our careers. We made the mistake of believing that we had to *be* our careers.'

Unlike Kate, the way Emma and I view ourselves and where we fit in the world has been so limited. 'I increasingly feel that my life is filled with opportunities,' Kate says. 'My impression of life is that it can offer me so much more than I thought it could a few years ago.'

Winter

'Now is the winter of our discontent'
– William Shakespeare

23

UNIVERSAL SUFFERING

Despite my new hope that one day I could be 40-something and into it too, my current discontentment feels like a low-grade infection. To Chris's relief I've started cooking again, but no matter what I do or how I distract myself, dissatisfaction is always flowing through my veins. Sometimes it spikes into overwhelming despair, mostly in response to the Sunday Night Blues at the thought of going back to work on Monday. Some weeks the Sunday Night Blues start as early as Saturday afternoon, and the discontentment virus takes hold of my body for most of the weekend.

I have worked out what I don't want any more. I don't want to spend the best part of my life wearing pinstripes, talking shit and pretending that I care. But even if I had the financial means to cut corporate-Kasey loose, talking to Peter has made me realise that it still wouldn't be enough. The formula for my happiness is more complicated than just removing the things I don't like. Nor is it enough to just start doing more things that I do like. I've come to the conclusion that the source of meaning and fulfilment is as much internal as it is external. I wonder if perhaps one of the things missing in my life is spirituality.

Don't worry: this book is not about to take a drastic turn through Religionland and how I found God. I'm not even sure if I believe in God. I was raised an agnostic. I've never been christened, and the few times I've been in a church for weddings and funerals have been immensely stressful – I had no idea when to stand or kneel.

But the more I read about happiness and fulfilment the more I discover the correlation between spirituality and well-being. It seems almost every happiness study ever conducted concludes that, on the whole, people who are religious or spiritual are happier than those who are not.

I've often felt a little envious of religious people because they seem to get something out of it that I don't understand. I wonder if I might be missing out on something. Having said that, it doesn't feel right to just cherry-pick a religion. It seems a bit opportunistic to sign up to a religion as an adult in the hope that it will improve my well-being. I know this makes no sense at all; surely a choice you make as an adult is more valid than just inheriting the religion of your parents? Then again, maybe you need to start when you're young – too young to think about how faith works logically or rationally. While I understand how comforting it would be, I've always had a hard time believing in stories that deny the laws of nature. And if I can't believe in those elements, then any adoption of religion seems a bit half-arsed.

I imagine this is one of the reasons why Buddhism is so popular among adults in the Western world. On the whole, Buddhism doesn't ask believers to believe in the magical or superstitious elements. Reportedly, Buddhism has become particularly popular with corporate types like me.

This is going to sound really harsh, but all the people I know who have converted to Buddhism frustrate me. They all seem to fit the profile of ambitious, materialistic corporate types who re-decorate their houses with Tibetan tapestries and then start oozing moral superiority. I find it really unattractive, to say nothing of their choices for soft furnishings. From what I can tell, they don't seem to have any sense of community or the common good other than being nice to people just to ensure Karma doesn't revisit them and bite them on the arse. If that's how they want to live their lives, then fine, but to act as if they are morally superior when all they are doing is taking out a Karmic insurance policy rubs me the wrong way.

I'm sure there must be more to Buddhism than what I have witnessed from my recently converted colleagues and associates. I suspect some of them have only adopted the elements of Buddhism that fit conveniently with Western culture. Elizabeth Gilbert, author of *Eat, Pray, Love*, who earned her spiritual street cred in an ashram in India, did a better job of selling the merits of Buddhism. Not only did she write about her spiritual journey so exquisitely it almost made me sick with envy – not a very Buddhist response, I'm sure – she also detailed how meditation helped her tame her internal demons and discontent.

This sounds just what I need, but, unlike Elizabeth Gilbert, my bank balance won't allow me to jump on a plane to India. With much pride, and even more relief, I have paid off my credit-card debt, and I'm not about to max it out again with a trip to Bombay. In addition, I spent a week in India a few years ago for work, and it was the most horrific travel experience I've ever had. I have no intention of going back any time soon. The poverty and desperation in India made me sick to the core. I spent a few years growing up in Indonesia, so I'd seen poverty and gross inequality in living standards before, but nothing could have prepared me for the horror of India. Parents chopping off the arms and legs of their children so they get more money begging is just beyond what I can cope with.

I know people say India is a spiritual place, but I can't imagine how they can look past the brutal poverty to find any peace and tranquillity. Consequently, I decide to look into meditation options within the comfort and pleasantness of my privileged Western existence. I also don't want to invest three months in a process I'm not sure will work for me. I look for a just-add-water, quick-fix, jump-in-the-deep-end meditation experience. I find it in a Vipassana course – a ten-day silent meditation practice.

Vipassana catches my attention because it claims to be non-sectarian. I'm not required to sign up to any group or believe in anything that defies the laws of physics or reason – no worshipping, no gods, no miracles. It is also universal in that it is complementary to all religions, nationalities and ethnicities. S.N. Goenka, the teacher in charge, says that suffering and misery are universal. No matter what part of the globe we come from, or what we believe in, we all experience misery the same way. Therefore the solution to suffering should also be universal. Vipassana isn't about praying, hoping or writing gratitude diaries to manifest the things we want in our lives. The basic premise is that shit happens in life and the only way to end our misery is to learn not to react to the shit. No matter how we live our lives, there will always be external events that either don't happen when we want them to or happen when we least want them. The only thing we can control is our internal response to these events. By learning to manage our internal responses we not only end our suffering, we also become more compassionate and better human beings.

What I read on the various websites sounds good enough for me to give it a try. I am also impressed that it is run solely on donations and volunteer labour. Goenka learned Vipassana in his 20s when he was searching for a cure to his migraines. He was a rich businessman living in Burma at the time and had consulted medical experts all over the world in an attempt to find a cure. As a last resort, he tried Vipassana, a 2,500-year-old technique. Not only did it cure his migraines, it also eradicated the discontent and meaninglessness of his rich corporate existence. Over time, he has set up Vipassana Meditation Centres all over the world, and they are all resourced by the goodwill of the meditators and community. It seems that Goenka also did what Caroline the coach recommended to me – he harnessed his skills and experience as a businessman and entrepreneur to apply them in a new situation to create something better.

It all sounds so good that I fill out the online application form and eagerly wait for a reply. Weeks pass before I receive an email from the Vipassana Meditation Centre informing me that they've rejected my application.

The bastards rejected me. A bunch of lentil-eating, sandal-wearing, social-fringe-dwelling hippies rejected me. Compassionate – my arse. They are just as compassionate as the other opportunistic, moralistic Karmic recruits I know.

On the registration form, I was asked to disclose my age, profession, medical history and current physical and mental health. I hate questions about mental health. I always worry that once people find out I had PTSD and depression they'll conclude that I'm nuts. I considered lying on the form, because, let's face it, it's not like they would ever be able to find out. But given that Buddhists are supposed to be open-minded and compassionate I decided to tell the truth. I should have lied. They rejected my application based on their concern for my mental health.

I send them an email asking them to reconsider. I explain that my mental health problems occurred a long time ago and, given all the therapy and self-reflection I've gone through, I am far tougher emotionally than I've ever been. They reconsider my application and agree to let me attend. Perhaps they aren't as compassionless as I first thought.

You'd think that I would be happy about being accepted into the course. I've convinced them to let me attend and got what I wanted. But my first thought is, 'Oh shit, now I have to do it.' Even though I was outraged by the rejection, I was secretly quite pleased about it. I am terrified of what lies ahead of me, and having them reject me was an easy way out. Now if I am going to chicken out, the responsibility will be mine alone.

The only other time I've been locked away for an extended period of time was when I went to an old convent in Holland to learn Dutch – twelve hours of Dutch lessons every day for two weeks. It was hell.

I moved to Holland without speaking a word of Dutch. I naively thought that Dutch people speak English so it wasn't necessary for me to speak Dutch. It didn't occur to me that although Dutchies speak English they prefer to speak Dutch.

After I'd been in Holland for a couple of months and made little progress with learning the language, my company sent me off to the convent. It is an intensive language school that was set up by the nuns in Holland's Golden Era to teach the sailors languages before they went off on their voyages. Now it's just a very expensive and very intensive language school for business people and rich kids flunking their language classes at school.

As my company paid for me to attend the course, I was keen to show them that they had got their money's worth when I returned. I asked one of the teachers to teach me how to say 'I work for a pipe company.' I practised it at the weekend and on Monday over lunch I demonstrated my language skills to one of the directors of my company. I said that I worked for a '*pijpen bedrijve*'.

The room went silent as soon as the words left my mouth, and everybody stared at me. It wasn't until later that my secretary pulled me aside to tell me that while '*pijpen*' did mean pipe originally, it is now commonly understood to mean blowjob. What else did they expect from a convent?

When I was with the nuns, I cried every day. With the Buddhists, it is no different.

24

SILENCING THE LITTLE BITCH

On the drive up to the Vipassana Meditation Centre, it occurs to me that I know nothing about these people. Despite what I've read on the websites, for all I know they could be some freaky religious sect that entices gullible people with the promise of spiritual enlightenment and then chops them up into little pieces as a form of human sacrifice. I ask Chris to keep an eye on the news for any reports of mass suicides or bizarre rituals. He puts a reassuring hand on my knee and says, 'You'll be OK, puss cat.'

I say an emotional goodbye to Chris at the gate of the centre and feel like I am going off to war. My stomach turns when I read the sign on the gate stating that visitors cannot enter until 6.30 a.m. on the 11th day. My uneasy feeling intensifies when I go inside to register and see that they are taking people's car keys off them. We really are stuck here. They are also confiscating our books, writing material, mobile phones, iPods, cigarettes and medication.

I glance around the room at the other human sacrifices and feel grossly inadequate. Am I the only person who didn't know to wear the uniform consisting of Birkenstocks and Thai fisherman pants? I am instantly taken back to the playground and fear that the other meditators won't play with me at lunchtime because I am wearing an embroidered lacy dress. Then I think, 'What do I care? We aren't allowed to speak to each other anyway.'

After I register and relinquish everything in my possession that goes beep, I find my dormitory and meet my roommates. We are still allowed to speak, so I introduce myself and ask them all why they've come.

Sally is a 30-year-old personal assistant to a couple of executives. She is on a personal development journey and has come to the Vipassana course out of curiosity. She is a big fan of Anthony Robbins, the American self-help guru and motivational speaker, telling everyone in the room that he is a gift from God and has the purest heart out of anybody she's ever known. I ask her what she's learned from Saint Anthony, and she says, 'To be true to my core.' I hold my tongue when she talks about the merits of that horrible self-help book *The Secret* and wonder why she needs Vipassana if she is already 'true to her core' and capable of manifesting anything she wants. Wouldn't you just manifest the benefits of Vipassana and skip the ten days of silence?

Jo, the 29-year-old architect who proudly tells me she rolls her own cigarettes, has come in the hope that meditation will help with her insomnia. She says she hasn't slept for years, and quitting smoking will be an added bonus. Helen is 25 and works in an advertising agency. She can't articulate why she has come but speaks a lot about how much she loves her job. She loves the stress, fast pace and being able to wear stilettos to work. I think, 'Enjoy it while it lasts, sista.' And Kelly the 31-year-old teacher is here because several of her friends had done the course and claimed it had changed their lives. Her friends had done the course several years ago, but Kelly wanted to wait until she was in a happy place in her life before she tried it. She doesn't want to use it as an escapist exercise, and since she's just got married and feels very settled she thinks now is a good time.

One of Kelly's friends didn't complete the course. She was sent home in disgrace halfway through because she was caught shagging one of the other meditators. Not only had Kelly's friend broken the rule of 'sexual misconduct', she also broke the rule of going outside the camp boundaries. Perhaps in response to such past indiscretions, the management have instituted a total gender segregation at the centre for the duration of the course. The only time we see the boys is in the meditation hall. But even then we have separate entrances and we sit at opposite sides of the hall.

The rationale behind the segregation is to remove any sensual or sexual distraction. I am amused by how heterosexual this rule is – we're not allowed to look at men, but we share bedrooms with women. The Dalai Lama is quoted as saying that in Buddhism homosexuality is considered to be sexual misconduct. Perhaps this is why; otherwise, removing total sexual distraction would be a logistical nightmare.

The briefing session on the first evening outlines the timetable for the next ten days. Wake up at 4 a.m., meditate from 4.30 a.m. to 9 p.m. and go to bed at 9.30 p.m. Every day! For ten days! We will break for breakfast at 6.30 a.m. and lunch at 11 a.m. There will be no eating after midday, though new students are allowed to eat fruit at 5 p.m. if they wish. I wish, my God do I wish.

Jo the architect has a stomach ulcer, so she is allowed to eat a proper meal in the evenings. It's amazing how appetising brown rice and salad can be when you're hungry. Every night as I sit in the dining room munching on my apple I wish I had a stomach ulcer, too.

After the introductory briefing, we take a vow of Noble Silence. This means no communication in any form: no talking, no eye contact, no interaction at all. We are allowed to ask questions of the teacher for five minutes at lunchtime and again at 9 p.m., and if we have a practical question like needing a bar of soap we can speak to the manager. Other than that we are on our own.

I only break Noble Silence on one occasion and am promptly scolded for it. I ask a girl in my room to open the door at night to let in some fresh air. She says she can't because the fly screen has holes in it, which will let mosquitoes in. Since we are on Buddhist soil, we can't kill the little bastards, so I suggest she puts socks in the holes. The manager is nowhere in sight during this conversation, but the next thing I know she rushes over and reminds me of my vow of Noble Silence. I feel like I am on school camp.

Other than being very inconvenient when it comes to sorting out practicalities, Noble Silence is unbelievably lonely – far lonelier than I had expected. I crave the warmth and stimulation of human interaction – a welcoming glance, a reassuring smile. My loneliness is most acute at lunchtime as I walk around the garden crying, and then at night when I lie in bed wishing Chris into my arms. My tears aren't violent or torrential. I'm not even sure what I am crying about. Yet every lunchtime and every night, without fail, my eyes fill with soft, gentle tears. Sleeping is impossible. Just like Wilbur in *Charlotte's Web*, it's hard to sleep when your tummy is empty and your head is full.

Even worse than the loneliness is listening to the little bitch inside my head – the one who is always the first to point out that I'm not good enough, not clever enough, not pretty enough, not thin enough. With nobody else's voice to drown her out, she takes centre stage in my mind and drives me nuts. By day three, I am ready to kill her. As time goes on, though, she starts to shut up, and by the last couple of days I hardly hear her at all. When she does speak, she isn't nasty any more; we may even have become friends. It is such a relief to gag the bitch.

25

SENSATIONAL

H ave you any idea how boring it is to focus on the bottom of your nose for 13 hours a day?

We spend the first three days of the Vipassana course 'sharpening our mind' so as to detect all the different sensations in our bodies and have the concentration to focus on them. In practice, this means focusing on the little bit of skin between the bottom of the nose and the top of the lip.

I've only been here a couple of hours when my mind starts screaming at me, 'You can't spend the next ten days of your life focusing on one square inch of flesh. You're not that fucked up.'

As the hours pass, I can feel myself getting better at detecting the sensation of my breath passing in and out of my nose, but I cannot get my mind to focus for more than a couple of breaths at a time. I think about all sorts of things, ranging from all the people who have ever wronged me in my life to how much I want to shag Chris and what I should do with my life. But most of all, I keep thinking about all the reasons why I should leave. I start pattern matching: Goenka's got a fat gut, Buddha's got a fat gut, if I stay here I'll get a fat gut, too.

Apparently this kind of focus taps into your subconscious and starts loosening up all the baggage and issues. Goenka says that our mind wanders because we are trying to distract ourselves from the painful reality that lies deep within us. I must have a lot of baggage, because my mind is constantly distracted with thoughts of going home. Despite trying to tell myself that it's only ten days of my life and I can put up with anything for ten days, I want to run from the place screaming. If I weren't so proud, I probably would have.

Sally, the loyal disciple of Anthony Robbins, leaves halfway through the first day. When I see her being escorted out of the gate, my first reaction is envy. I assume her mind has wandered onto a good enough reason to leave; I don't think she's been there long enough to shag anybody. I'm not surprised when she leaves. Vipassana is the antithesis of Anthony Robbins. There is no rock concert hype or grandstand chanting of 'Every day in every way I'm getting more enlightened'.

I've never been to one of his events, though I have listened to some of his CDs and watched countless infomercials, and from what I can tell Anthony Robbins is about instantly energising people and making them feel good about themselves, whereas Vipassana requires a lot of hard work and pain before you get any pay-off. I'm starting to realise that the benefits of Vipassana are enduring in a way that motivational hype is not. In my experience, the hype and buzz of motivational speakers wears off before you get out of the stadium car park. I suppose that's why it's such a successful business model. People have to keep coming back to get another hit of Personal Mastery.

Another woman leaves on the fourth day. This surprises me because on day four it starts to get interesting – and more painful. For three hours a day, we are not allowed to move. Sitting as still as a Buddha statue with your back straight and your legs crossed becomes unbelievably painful. At times, I am so overcome with physical and emotional pain I think I am going to be sick. In fact, the lady sitting in front of me is sick. I feel sorry for the men, being naturally less flexible than the women. If it is painful for me, it must be excruciating for them.

As well as sitting still, we also learn the technique of Vipassana meditation. I am relieved to discover there is more to it than just staring at your nose. It involves scanning your body to detect all the different sensations and then learning to be objective and 'equanimous' to all of them. This means that whether the sensation is pleasurable or painful you need to keep a neutral, detached mind. The purpose behind this is learning not to develop cravings for the good sensations or aversion to the painful ones. It's based on the Buddhist principle that all life is suffering and that suffering is caused by cravings for things you want or developing aversions to things you don't want. When you liberate yourself from cravings and aversions, you liberate yourself from suffering. So when I've been sitting still for hours dripping in sweat, feeling like I've been run over by a truck and dipped in salt, I'm supposed to observe my pain with equanimity. Another part of maintaining equanimity is not caring about the reason you feel the sensation – be it from a previous physical injury, the strain of sitting still, or an emotional sensation. A sensation is a sensation, is a sensation.

This is the theory anyway. It proves to be a lot harder to maintain my objectivity in practice.

With a sharper mind from the three days of staring at my nose, I am able to scan my body and detect all sorts of sensations. The pain is pretty easy to detect, but I can also feel subtle vibrations running up and down my body. At night when I lie in bed I am vibrating so much I feel like a tuning fork. Sometimes I feel like there is electricity running through my body and at other times it is like ants are crawling over me.

After a while, I work out the link between emotions and physical sensations. When I think about something upsetting and a painful or unpleasant emotion arises, I can detect a corresponding sensation in my body. After a couple of days, I work out that an emotion is in fact just a physical sensation. And since I am able to endure the pain of sitting still, I become more confident that I can endure the sensations of painful emotions.

On the eighth day, my black dog pads into the meditation hall and places an oppressive paw on my shoulder. The grey clouds he always brings with him weigh down on me. They are so thick I can hardly breathe – it is going to be bad this time. Then I remember the principles of Vipassana. I turn to him and say, 'Hey, big fella, I haven't seen you for a while.' He digs his claws into my shoulder, and searing pain shoots through my body. 'Don't you want to know why I came?' he asks.

I do my best to observe the pain with equanimity and say, 'No, thanks, that's not important to me any more.' He bares his teeth and growls at me menacingly. I say, 'Look, buddy, you can stay if you want, but you'll have to observe Noble Silence like the rest of us. It's not all about you, you know.' I continue on with my meditation, trying to focus on all the other sensations in my body. After about an hour I notice that he has gone and he's taken the grey clouds with him. Big clumsy equanimous tears roll down my cheeks as I realise, 'Holy shit, this really works.'

That night as I lie in bed observing my tummy rumbling, I think about my black dog and understand that I don't need to be scared of him any more. Up until now, my depression has always overwhelmed me. It felt like it consumed my entire being, and I lived in constant fear that when it came it would stay for an eternity. After objectively observing depression in the meditation hall, I now realise that it does not consume my whole being. In reality, what I feel is heaviness on my head and shoulders and tightness around my stomach. It is a revelation that emotional pain is in fact just physical sensations, no different from the pains in my back and knees I've been feeling for the seven days prior. And after sitting through and surviving all those other sensations I know that all pain eventually passes away and that I'm strong enough to deal with it.

Right about now you're probably saying to yourself, 'She's lost it. That's way too simplistic.' And I can't fault you. It used to frustrate the hell out of me when people told me to deal with depression and anxiety by 'witnessing' it. How was I supposed to be the audience and the actor at the same time, especially when I was in the depths of an attack? I was incapable of being objective about anything, let alone myself. But now I've experienced it. Now I get it.

I'm sure my black dog will come again, but I also know how to observe the heaviness and tightness with equanimity until he leaves. I can't tell you how liberated and empowered this makes me feel.

The next day, I have a similar experience, but this time it is with anger. While I am meditating, thoughts of my parents flood into my mind. I think about what they've put me through in the last few years since their divorce and how I have suffered. I am consumed by rage, but once again I observe the sensations. My jaw tenses, my hands shake and my stomach burns. I objectively observe the sensations until they pass, but then start feeling ridiculous. By making the connection between emotions and physical sensations I realise how I am perpetuating my own suffering by maintaining my anger at my parents. When I get angry at them, I'm the one that feels like shit, not them; they don't even know. It seems so futile to keep making myself feel bad, so I resolve to let go of my anger and resentment.

Halfway through the tenth day, we are allowed to talk. I'd heard that after ten days of silence and physically demanding meditation, the emotional release would be so intense it would be euphoric. A massive orgasm was the precise metaphor. If there is such a thing as a bad orgasm, I experience it at that moment. As people leave the meditation hall chatting and laughing, I am overwhelmed with emotion and despair. I avoid everybody and go straight to the toilets and cry gut-wrenching sobs.

Sitting all alone on cold porcelain, I feel like I am reliving all the physical and emotional pain I've ever suffered in my life in one fell swoop. The backdrop of chatter and laughter from the other meditators makes my distress all the more acute. I seek out the assistant teacher to tell him how I feel, and he says what he always says: that I should observe the sensations with equanimity. I tell him, probably a little too forcefully, that I understand the theory but when everybody else is elated I feel like I've been cheated out of the return on my investment. Surely I didn't just endure ten days of hell to feel like shit at the end of it?

He says, 'Your mind has just undergone ten days of very deep surgery. I believe you understand the technique well, so your incision has been very deep. When you cut into something that is infected, pus will come out. It's painful when the pus comes out, but it's necessary to heal. The wound may be raw for a couple of days. Give it time.'

At the end of the tenth day, Goenka gives a talk about how we should maintain the practice of meditation. In ten days, all we have done is plant a seed of peace and happiness. Meditation is a life-long practice and to do it properly we need to meditate for two hours every day.

What? I've just put myself through all of that to come out with only a seed? I don't want a bloody seed. I want enlightenment. I feel ripped off for a moment until I realise that it took me eighteen years to acquire my academic education, so it seems a little unrealistic to obtain spiritual enlightenment in only ten days. On two occasions during the course, though, I glimpsed spiritual enlightenment. It was only for a moment, but it was enough for me to understand what it is and convince me that I want it.

On the eighth day just before my black dog came, and again on the ninth day, I felt myself leave my body. All of a sudden, I noticed that I was observing myself and everything around me from outside my body. In those moments, I could no longer feel the sensations in my body; in fact, I couldn't feel anything. It was more like knowing than feeling. For a brief moment I *knew* love, peace and everything. Or maybe even I *was* love, peace and everything. But as soon as I'd registered what was happening I was back in my body, back in the pain and sweat of the meditation hall. It was so brief and is so difficult to describe that part of me wants to believe I imagined it or maybe just passed out from the pain. But somehow I just know.

It would be easy to be intoxicated by and crave this transcendental experience, but according to Goenka you can't obtain it if you crave it. You have to be beyond craving and beyond aversion: in a state of equanimity. It seems like the ultimate paradox – the more you want it, the more it eludes you. I think he might be right, because it hasn't happened to me again. And even though I know I have to not want it, I really do. It seems I have a way to go before my seed blossoms into the tree of enlightenment.

Vipassana meditation is also supposed to make you more loving and compassionate. Maybe it worked a little, but it is obvious to me on day ten that I've yet to master this compassion thing. After I finish sobbing in the toilet, I go into the dining room to chat with the other meditators. The first person I speak to is a middle-aged man I'd noticed every day because during the times we were unable to move he started breathing loudly like he was in labour. He says he is dying to know how the stock market is going and then proceeds to list off all his assets. Before I can stop myself, I think, 'You fuckwit.' Then I remember I am supposed to be sharing love and compassion with all beings, so I politely excuse myself. This compassion thing is clearly going to take some time.

On the last night, I overhear some of the guys talking in their room. It seems that after their intense spiritual journeys the only thing they can speak about is sex. I'm not speaking about it, but I am certainly thinking about it. After eating something fried, it is the first thing I want to do when I get home. With heightened awareness of my physical sensations, sex is amazing. Maybe the euphoric orgasmic experience promised at the end of the course is intended to be literal rather than metaphoric. Regardless, there is no way I am equanimous to that.

I can't tell you how good it is to see Chris again. It feels like we've been apart for months rather than days. Although, when he comes to pick me up, I get into the car and instead of telling him how much I missed him I say, 'I want to have a baby.' The words just pop out of my mouth as if they bypassed my brain. 'I don't know where that came from,' I say. 'I swear, I have no idea why I just said that.'

Chris smiles at me knowingly. 'I'm not surprised,' he says. 'You're so maternal. You're maternal with Toffee, with Michael, with your friends. The only one who doesn't see it is you. Maybe you needed ten days of reflection to work out what the rest of us already knew.' And then he says, 'You'd make a great mother.'

I am surprised how touched I am by the compliment, and I feel my eyes well with tears. I blink them away and say, 'I thought you didn't want kids.'

'I'm open to having kids,' Chris says. 'I just thought that you didn't want them. And if I have to choose between having you and having kids, I choose you.'

We agree to talk about it again in a year.

26

THE EPIPHANY

So did Vipassana change my life? Were all those hours of concentrating, hurting and sweating worth it?

I walk away from the ten days without the epiphany I was hoping for. I don't find the single answer to what I should do with my life to get total meaning and fulfilment. I don't find my give-a-shit. But other people do. One lady tells me with tears in her eyes that she has been searching for 40 years for answers and now she has them. The only problem is she wasn't able to articulate them, so I can't share them with you.

Some other people claim, when I speak to them a few months later, that it has improved their marriages; others credit it with helping them run faster and longer; while others say it helped them lose weight. I lost weight too, but that was from not eating dinner for ten days.

One guy who attended the course with me did so in order to deal with his anger and feelings of rejection about being adopted. He sat his first course two years previously, after he had an emotional meltdown. He was pretty messed up after meeting his birth mother for the first time and dealt with it through drinking, smoking pot and fighting with his wife. He says the first course made him a lot more aware of how he was reacting to things in his life, and he left feeling a lot less angry. For the first six months after the course, he felt wonderful: he stopped drinking and smoking and was getting along with his family.

But he says that after about nine months the benefits had worn off and he reverted back to being a grumpy bastard. So his wife had sent him back to do the course again. After the second course, she says it seems like he has released a lot of anger.

One of the best ways to describe the course is an emotional detox. Almost everybody I speak to says they freed themselves from negative emotions, be it anger, guilt, jealousy or fear. I can understand now why my application was rejected initially. In order to detox those emotions, you have to be prepared to feel them and deal with them. The course is incredibly confronting emotionally, and if you aren't on top of your game it would be very difficult to endure. One of the meditators on my course is a psychiatrist, and she says that she would strongly discourage anybody suffering from a severe mental illness from doing the course. She says in those cases it can be very damaging to focus inwards and expose yourself to even more pain.

I have also changed my mind about Buddhism being a selfish endeavour. The focus of meditation is to help yourself, but the end goal is to help others. It is the opposite, from what I know, of Christianity, which teaches that by helping other people you become a better person and therefore help yourself. Buddhism comes at it from the other direction, claiming that if you work on fixing yourself you become less angry, less reactive and more compassionate, which in turn helps other people. This makes sense to me now. My actions are now less driven by reactions to things. Events that would have previously annoyed me don't bother me any more, so I don't tend to react in ways that are inflammatory.

I wish I could tell you that I've mastered compassion, but I haven't. I still find myself being critical and judgemental of other people, but I think I do it less now than I used to. Sometimes when people are acting badly, rather than thinking they are pricks I find myself thinking they could benefit from ten days of Vipassana.

I'm also less critical about myself. I used to wake up every morning and look in the mirror and see acne scars and wrinkles. Now I look in the mirror and say to myself, 'You're hot.' My friend Jules recommends looking in the mirror and saying out loud, 'You're so sexy, I'd do you.' Apparently the more people who are around to hear it, the more satisfying it is. I can't quite bring myself to do that, but my inner voice is certainly a whole lot nicer to me than she was before.

I have continued to meditate at home. I don't do it every day, but I sit a few times a week. I find that at the end of the session I have amazing clarity of thought. Every time I meditate, I feel like I'm topping up my inner peace and harmony.

And one day when I am least expecting it, as I am sitting on my meditation cushion at home, it all falls into place. The epiphany I was looking for pops into my mind. It just isn't what I was expecting and is somewhat underwhelming.

My epiphany is . . . impermanence. As I sit there observing the sensations in my body, I finally understand the concept of impermanence and what that means to my life. All sensations, the good, bad and euphoric, have the same characteristic: they arise, stay for a time and then pass away. I transpose this concept into my life and into my search for meaning and fulfilment and realise that even if I do find 'The answer' it will only be 'The answer' for a time. I will change, it will change and the world will change. Just as management consulting used to rock my world and now bores me silly, the next answer I find will also change over time.

I probably would have come to this realisation by myself eventually, because both Caroline and Kate had said the same thing. But somehow I needed to feel it for myself before I understood it. And just like them, this realisation takes the pressure off me. I don't need to look for something that is big enough and important enough to sustain me for ever. I don't need to look for one monolithic answer. All I need to find is the next lily pad to jump to. And then when I've finished with that one I can jump to the next one. Rather than standing still, getting frustrated and disenchanted waiting for the very best lily pad to come along like Peter is doing, maybe it's better to take a risk and just jump. It's not even that much of a risk, because that lily pad is impermanent and sooner or later I'll have to jump to the next one anyway.

I met a barrister doing the Vipassana course who is just about to jump to her next lily pad. Sophie is a very impressive woman. She is strong, articulate, grounded and spends her days playing hardball in a man's world. Initially she was attracted to law for the glamour and prestige. After doing her time as a solicitor, she decided to become a barrister because going to court seemed so much more exciting than doing paperwork. Sophie worked hard and sacrificed a lot to get where she is, but now she is also 30-something and over it.

'I feel like I've entered a different phase of my life where a career is not the only option for me,' she says. 'I want to take a breath and enjoy life. I want to live life a different way.

'Being a barrister is very stressful. Once you are involved in a trial it becomes your whole life. People bring their toothbrushes into the office and just camp out until the trial is over.' Sophie doesn't want to live like that any more. 'I'm slowing down. I'm not as ambitious as I used to be, and I'm interested in having children. This is not a good job for relationships.'

She's also over the boys' club, the egos and the competitiveness, and has lost her faith in the law. 'I don't believe it's about achieving justice for people. It is so subject to human error. Sometimes I'll get somebody off, and I'll think, "You did it, you so did it."'

When Sophie realised she wasn't fighting as hard as she normally would, and that being right and winning didn't matter to her any more, she decided that she needed to try something new.

She has enrolled in a journalism course at university. In the entrance interview for the course, she was warned what to expect as a rookie journalist. Most likely she'll start off writing stories about the local football team or a boy who rescued a cat stuck up in a tree. Her income will be pitiful compared with what she earns as a barrister. I ask her if she is prepared for that. She says her decision to study journalism is not about moving directly into a new career but a step towards learning new skills to do the things she enjoys in life. 'It's about exploration and discovery at this stage in my life transition,' she says. 'I am happy to play life by ear. It's not about career at all any more. I simply want to live, feel alive and be well, engaged and spirited.'

I ask Sophie what Vipassana has taught her. She says she has realised that life 'is not about happiness, it's about being more peaceful and calm. Happiness is very temperamental.'

27

MADAM BARBARA

Emma has started her wandering phase. Instead of spending hours at the pet shop like I am, she tells her colleagues she has off-site meetings with clients and suppliers and spends her days in cafés, shops and parks. She rings me one afternoon in distress. 'You wouldn't believe the number of people in the park in the middle of the day,' she says. 'Surely they aren't all mothers and shift workers. They must all work for themselves, and they all look happy. What am I doing, Kase? I want to be self-employed and happy too.'

In desperation, Emma suggests we go to the Mind, Body and Spirit Exhibition in search of inspiration. She is even more sceptical than I am about dolphins and magic. We once saw a car bumper sticker saying 'Magic Happens' and Emma's response was 'So does cot death.' So her suggestion that we look to the New Age movement highlights how desperate she is becoming to solve her 30-something crisis.

We go there searching for answers. What we find is an industry peddling pretty things to vulnerable people.

I walk from stall to stall feeling agitated and uncomfortable, but I can't put my finger on what is bothering me. Emma nails it. 'Look at the people here,' she says. 'They are borderline underprivileged and they are shelling out hundreds of pounds on lavender oil and angel statues hoping it will change their lives.'

She is right. The clientele are not members of the wealthy elite who have money to burn. This isn't just a fun day out; there is desperation in the air, mixing with the scent of patchouli and lavender. I worry that some of these people are exchanging the housekeeping money for a dream – a simple solution that cannot possibly fix any sort of complex problem. This isn't nurturing 'mind, body and spirit'; it is exploitation.

We sit in a seminar where a woman who has recently been crowned 'Witch of the Year' talks about how a combination of crystals and the advice in the books she has written (which are all on sale at the back of the room for £15 each or three for £40) will change our lives. I feel sick when a woman in the audience asks if this will help her heal from her abusive childhood, hostile divorce and wayward son. This woman doesn't need to spend £100 on stones and workbooks. She needs counselling from a trained psychologist and not affirmations from the Witch of the Year.

The highlight for me is the advertisement for tantric sex. It offers a one-hour one-on-one 'tutorial' with a Tantric Goddess for men or a one-hour massage for women. Great, so the men get a shag, and the women get a massage. Top marks for attempting to turn prostitution into a spiritual experience.

The exhibition is held opposite a casino complex, and I can't help but notice the irony. Despite the tie-dyed purple kaftans, the dreadlocks and earth-mother emblems, these people are as ruthlessly commercial as the casino operator selling gambling chips to pensioners. On both sides of the road, people are risking their hard-earned cash on a quick-fix solution. And on both sides of the road, people are profiting from selling escapism and false hope. The New Age industry is as addictive as the slot machines – up-selling and cross-selling every step along the path to enlightenment.

Perhaps Emma and I have inhaled too deeply and are starting to believe that magic can happen. Despite our scepticism, we decide to seek the guidance of a clairvoyant – a wise woman with a hotline to the universe.

My one and only previous experience with a clairvoyant did not do much to enhance the reputation of the profession. I went with my friend Robert, who was studying to be a doctor at the time. Robert didn't have much money with him, so we told the clairvoyant that he was unemployed and asked for a discount. She generously agreed to give him a reading at half price, but then spent the entire time talking about the job offer coming his way very soon. According to the spirit guides, he would soon be offered a job as a labourer. In utter defiance of the universe's predetermination, Robert completed the last three years of his medical degree without once having the opportunity to shout 'Show us your tits' from the top of scaffolding.

Madam Barbara has been recommended to Emma by a friend. The friend credits Madam Barbara's readings with changing her life and helping her to get pregnant. Maybe she can help us conceive our metaphorical babies.

As soon as I meet Madam Barbara, I can see why she has come so highly recommended. Just being in her presence is comforting and soothing. I can feel her energy radiating like warm sunlight on a crisp morning. It is hard to tell her age. She has lines on her face that would have taken 70 years to develop, but her eyes sparkle like those of a curious child. She is dressed in a free-flowing purple skirt and wears a jewelled ring on every finger. What is it with New Age people and purple?

I look over her shoulder as she greets me at the door of her home and see a pile of dirty purple clothes in a basket at the back of the house. I suppose even clairvoyants must concern themselves with domestic practicalities, although sitting in her reading room it would be easy to think that she could be exempt.

I could live my whole life in her reading room. Red velvet walls, big comfy cushions, water trickling over white stones, essential oil wafting in the air – it is so soothing and cosy, like a grown-up's version of the womb.

Emma has already seen Madam Barbara, but we have agreed not

to reveal anything about ourselves or each other so we can more accurately judge the credibility of her reading. We agree to meet afterwards for a coffee to debrief.

Madam Barbara switches on her tape recorder and shuts her eyes. I sit there awkwardly, unsure if I am required to do anything. After a couple of minutes in silence, she gasps and her eyes spring open. I jump off the couch with fright. When it comes to creating drama, this lady is a pro. 'I see an enormous change in you, dear,' she says. 'It started within you, but it has the effect of changing things in your outer world, too. It is the death of the old and the birth of the new.'

I suppose she could be talking about anything, but I immediately think about my depression. Forcing my black dog into obedience training had felt like a rebirth. Gwyneth Lewis refers to depression as a death in her wonderful book *Sunbathing in the Rain*. I know exactly what she means. When I was in the thick of my depression, I felt like I'd lost myself. I'd lost my personality, my spirit, not to mention my humour. I tried all sorts of things to find myself again, thinking that once I found myself I'd be healed. Then one day I realised that I was never going to find myself again because that person didn't exist any more – she was dead. What I had been doing through all those painful months of self-reflection was creating a new self. I had created a Kasey who was stronger and healthier: somebody that I liked. I had given birth to a new me.

'You have so much of the green energy, dear,' Madam Barbara continues. 'You're a carer, the person who wants to help others, guide others. You need to do work that will help others in order to achieve soul satisfaction.'

She tells me that what I am doing at the moment is not what I'll always be doing, but we can't do anything in this life without money and for a little while I need to focus on the cash. 'We have to do this first before we can get on with what we really want to do,' she says.

She tells me not to be discontented with what I'm doing now. There will be three offers that will come in my current field of work which will take me higher up the ladder, but 'the big one is yet to come'.

She hands me the tarot cards and instructs me to think of a question I'd like to ask her but not to say it. I have to visualise the question and 'shuffle it into the pack'. My question is 'What should I do with my life?', so I visualise myself waking up in the morning and springing out of bed with a purpose and a smile. I may have visualised myself as a couple of kilos lighter and with a smoother complexion as well.

I hand her the cards, and she strokes them as if she is reading Braille. She looks directly into my eyes, her curious gaze turning piercing, and she says, 'You have to write.'

I look up at her excitedly as if she's just given me the answer I've spent the last few months seeking. Damn. I've just given something away. Sometimes I can be so transparent.

The sceptic in me thinks she is reading my signals and running with it. The believer in me who is so desperate for guidance gives her the benefit of the doubt when she says, 'You have to help people through the written word. You have a gift with writing, there is no doubt about that. It's very strong in you.'

She turns over the first card in the deck and shakes her head. The card represents an illusionary state. 'This is about your fear of failure,' she says. 'You fear that you're not good enough to do it. What if I fail? What if it doesn't work out? So what? Just brush yourself off and start all over again.'

She turns over another card and says that there is a lovely offer coming to me. It's coming from a female, and I will have to decide if I stay with what I'm doing or accept the offer. 'This cannot be chosen logically,' she says. 'It has to be chosen with your instincts – with your need rather than your logic.'

The only 'lovely offer' I've had lately from a woman was from Susan, my former client, when she was naked in her hotel room. And to the dismay of my voyeuristic friends I made a choice based on logic rather than instincts. I'll have to do better next time.

Madam Barbara advises me to take the offer because it is my destiny. 'Don't try to avoid it. You don't even have to look for it. Just accept the offer when it comes.'

I put my left hand on the deck and ask my question again, silently. She turns over another card. It represents the fear of being defeated.

Madam Barbara recommends I spend time saying affirmations to get rid of my illusionary state. This advice sounds a little too much like the crystals and workbooks from the Witch of the Year, so I give her the benefit of the doubt and assume she's momentarily picked up some interference from the universe.

'There is new money for you to be made in a new way, but you need to get rid of that fear of failure, dear,' she says.

'Bit of a worrier, aren't you?' she asks rhetorically when she looks at my palm. 'That's the fear of disappointment that you have.' She pats my hand in the same nurturing way my grandmother used to do. 'Why are you so fearful?' she asks. 'An intelligent girl like yourself, a good-looking girl with it all going for you, what the hell do you have to worry about? It's ridiculous.'

She examines my palm again and asks if there are any twins in my family. She sees me having two boys and they are very close together. 'You could have boy twins,' she says.

Chris gets the thumbs up from Madam Barbara. She says that I need to make sure that I don't neglect him. 'You're very intelligent,' she says. 'But you can't be all brain and no love, warmth and affection. He does need it, you know.' She tells me that I'm very well loved and recommends that I don't delay getting married.

Next comes the I-Ching. According to Madam Barbara, I-Ching is a way of letting me talk to me. She says it is very important to realise that it isn't her talking to me, but the messages will come from my higher self, the bit that is connected with all that is. She is just interpreting my messages to myself.

I hold coins in both hands, charging them with the Ying and the Yang, and then throw them on the table. I do this a couple of times, then Madam Barbara tells me what I am trying to tell myself.

'It won't come easily,' she says. 'You're going to have to work hard for it, but if you do work hard you will realise your own Tao, your path. Trust your ideas. Don't have doubts.'

According to Madam Barbara, I am instructing myself to stop doing what I'm currently doing because now is the time to be adventurous and to step into life with a purpose. I need to eliminate all my doubts, all my illusions, and clear away all the obstacles in my mind so I can let the light of understanding shine though me and help others with it. I never knew I could be so poetic.

I am also telling myself that I will have to work hard and not get much for it, but it will be worth it in the long run because I will be doing something great, not just for myself but also for humanity.

While I would love to believe that I am telling myself that I have a purpose in life, I am somewhat concerned by my delusions of grandeur. It is starting to sound like I am about to go into the Gaza Strip to negotiate peace – something far nobler than I have the ability or intention to do.

Madam Barbara adds her own opinion by saying, 'You're going to have to do it anyway – whether you think you're strong enough or want to or not. It's your destiny.'

I tell her it all sounds great, but I don't know what this path is that she keeps referring to. 'Follow your bliss and you'll be successful,' she says. 'You'll never be without. That doesn't mean you'll be extremely wealthy, but you'll always have enough to get by on, and that's all we need.'

When the hour is up, I ask Madam Barbara about her life. She's been a 'reader' since she was a child. 'I've always had this gift,' she says. 'There was a time when I thought I'd like to be a businesswoman for a change, so I invested my money, very unwisely, in a sandwich shop and a deli. In a year, I'd aged about ten years, because in the morning I was working early in the sandwich shop making bloody egg and bacon sandwiches and then closed the shop and worked in the deli until nine o'clock at night.'

She was making good money out of it but realised that it was not the way she wanted to live, so she sold the shops and went back to reading – what she was meant to do. 'I moved away from reading when I got too logical about it, and it was a mistake,' she says.

175

As I leave, Madam Barbara calls out to me, 'Start with your writing. You really should make a start with writing something that will help other people. It will unfold as you go along.'

REAL BABIES

I float into the café on a cloud. I feel just as you would expect to feel after spending an hour listening to somebody tell you that you've been earmarked by the universe to make a meaningful contribution to humanity.

Emma and I are joined at the café by Chris and Emma's mother Jenny, all eager to dissect our mystical experiences.

Emma and I discover that our readings were surprisingly similar. Madam Barbara had told us both that we are going through a period of transformation and are about to change our career paths. Neither of us is currently doing what we are supposed to be doing. Both of us are being held back by fear, and we are both going to receive an offer from a woman. The major difference is that while I am destined to use my 'writing gift' to help people, Emma is destined to run her own business.

Madam Barbara told Emma that she has a 'lovely strong aura' and that people with strong auras are leaders. 'I'd like to see you working for yourself,' she said. 'This is the big change coming up for you. I see you doing your own thing in your own way.'

Madam Barbara said that while Emma currently gets a lot of freedom in her work, it's not the same as 'doing it by yourself, for yourself, and receiving the goodies from the work you do.

'You are asking yourself, "Should I just go away from what I'm doing now completely or should I stick with it?" You should go away. You won't be happy until you are doing your own thing in your own way,' Madam Barbara said.

Chris is not convinced, claiming we've just paid Madam Barbara to make us feel good about ourselves. He says her statements are so general they could mean anything to anybody. I can see his point. Most of her statements were extremely broad and open to interpretation, and it was indeed soothing and encouraging to listen to her predictions. But what about her prediction about my writing? That isn't general. Chris says it only resonates with me because I want to hear it. I disagree. Of course I want to hear it: not only am I desperate for the answer to my crisis, it's also rather nice to be told that I'm gifted at something. But she could have told me I was gifted at anything. If she'd said that I was gifted at music or sports or maths, I would have thought it was ridiculous. What are the chances of her picking the one thing that I am passionate about?

I have been seduced by the notion of 'helping people through the written word'. While my quest for meaning has become unashamedly selfish – deliberately questioning and rejecting the expectations of society and searching for something that enriches *me* and fulfils *me* – the notion that I can do something that would also help other people is surprisingly intoxicating. While I love the idea of writing, I love it even more when I view it as an endeavour that is greater than myself.

Emma's mother Jenny has been listening patiently up until this point. She puts down her cappuccino and says, 'I don't know why you girls are going to all this trouble looking for answers when it is obvious what you need to do. You need to have babies. That's what you're meant to be doing at this time in your life.'

Emma shoots me a glance across the table. It is not the first time she has heard this. It is Jenny's favourite broken record. Jenny has been encouraging Emma to breed for years. I have always thought it strange that Jenny did such a good job of raising a talented, driven and worldly career woman, only to tell her to give it up and get knocked up. What was the point? But that was before my 30-something crisis when I still viewed motherhood as a character flaw. Now I am willing to consider that Jenny may have a point. I'm even willing to consider that Madam Barbara's prediction about my boy twins may be just as significant as my writing. But I don't tell Jenny that.

For Emma's sake, I also don't tell Jenny about my recent conversation with a psychologist about being 30-something and over it. I want to know whether he's noticed a level of 30-something discontent in his patients and how he treats it. To my dismay, his solution is the same as Jenny's – women need babies and without them there is a void that cannot properly be filled with any other substitute. He says that if a woman presents in his office who is in her mid-30s or older, and without a stable relationship or a child, he knows she is going to have serious issues that will take years to deal with. In some cases, a stable relationship is 'adequate' for a woman to feel fulfilled, but essentially we are animals, and the female of the species is meant to breed. I challenge him about Judy and Samantha, who have both told me that if they had their time over they wouldn't have kids. The psychologist replies, 'Sure, that's what they say, but I bet they also said they wouldn't give their kids back.' He is right: they both said that to me.

He tells me to read Erik Erikson, a psychologist who came up with the notion of life stages and what we need to do at each stage to be happy, fulfilled and functional. 'The seventh life stage is called "generativity vs stagnation", which often starts when people are in their 30s,' he says. Essentially Erikson claims that we all need to be needed and if we don't devote ourselves to caring for and passing on our skills and knowledge to the next generation we're going to be fucked up. Interestingly, the stage before, which happens in our 20s, seems to involve developing our identity through our career. It's nice to know I passed that stage. I seem to be stumbling on the next one, though.

Even though my opinion of motherhood has changed considerably in the past few months, and Chris and I have put the kid issue on the agenda in a year's time, the advice of Jenny, the psychologist and Erikson is not particularly comforting. I'm prepared to accept that having kids could be *one* answer to being 30-something and over it, but I don't want to accept that it is *the* answer. It seems so stiflingly predetermined to think that it doesn't matter who we are or what we did with our lives prior to this point, we all have to breed in the end.

You may be calling me a hypocrite at this point, and you'd be right. Why I am reluctant to accept this biological determinism when I am eager to lap up the predetermination from the universe channelled by Madam Barbara?

For starters, I imagine giving birth to a piece of writing as compared with a child would not be so painful that it requires an epidural, although some of my tortured artist friends might tell you differently. Writing also doesn't have to be a 20-year commitment. I've just come to the understanding about impermanence, realising that if I get sick of something I can just leave it and try something new. But kids seem pretty permanent to me. And a piece of writing isn't going to knock on my door one day and tell me how I fucked it up in the way a child might.

I'd also hate to think that all the women who can't have children are destined to be unfulfilled and unhappy. Surely evolution is not that cruel – or should I say society? We are told all our lives that we need to do everything else first – get an education, establish ourselves professionally, buy property – but by the time we've done all that our biological clocks have tocked. The older I get, the more I am witnessing the heartbreak of women around me who are unable to get pregnant. And the harsh reality in many cases is that they just left it too late. I've lost count of how many women I know who are undergoing IVF or have tried it without success. When I think of how physically and emotionally invasive the process is, and how low the success rate is, I wonder if Erikson could be right. Surely you would only subject yourself to the emotional rollercoaster and expense of IVF if you were absolutely desperate for a baby?

Maybe I'm kidding myself, but I like to think that my friend Godfrey's metaphorical baby is an adequate substitute for a real one. Surely a metaphorical baby can still meet the needs that Erikson talks about, such as devoting ourselves to and caring for something, and leaving some sort of legacy.

I decide to think more seriously about how I can devote myself to, and nurture, a writing 'baby' – something that could also help other people.

Spring

'No winter lasts forever; no spring skips its turn'
– Hal Borland

29

WRITER'S LEAVE

But what should I write about?

At the moment, this doesn't seem like the most important question to ask. What the writing is about is not nearly as important to me as the act of doing it. And the act of writing is not nearly as important as having a reason not to go to work every day.

Since I went cold turkey on my excessive consumerist lifestyle, I've managed to get my financial situation back in the black. My credit-card debt is a distant memory, and I am even saving money each month. After fiddling with my budget, I calculate that if I am really disciplined I can now afford to work part-time. If I am prepared to make sacrifices in my lifestyle, such as going out less often, not buying any clothes and not going on holidays, I can afford to conceive and nurture my writing baby.

Even though I realise how lucky I am to be in a financial position that enables me to live on a part-time income, the decision isn't easy. There is no fat left in my budget, and the idea of living on 'just enough' terrifies me. I can easily reconcile myself to sacrificing the luxuries in my life, but the idea of living without a financial safety net keeps me awake at night. I am sure Chris would look after me if I got into financial trouble, but he has his own lifestyle to support and freelancing is risky enough for one person without having to worry about two. And ever since my family fell apart I don't have their support to fall back on either. If life throws me a curve ball and I need to get more money, the only thing left that I could sacrifice is my mortgage. My income protection insurance policy states that if I am unable to work I will receive 75 per cent of my income. I could live on 75 per cent of my full-time income, but there is no way I could make my mortgage repayments and live on 75 per cent of a part-time income. This sounds dramatic, but in deciding to work part-time I have to be prepared to risk my home.

After many revisions to my pros and cons list, I decide to take the risk. Out of all the reasons I've written in the pros column the most persuasive is simply because I can. Most people in the world don't have the luxury to work part-time and indulge in the pursuit of a metaphorical baby. I do, so I decide to go for it.

I decide to write a book about identity management. Over the last couple of years, I've spent a lot of time consulting to organisations that are developing strategies for identity management. This ranged from working out the best way of issuing computer log-ins to staff, to combating Internet banking fraud, to issuing identity cards. Most people would find this subject area mind-numbingly boring, but it appeals to my inner dark side. I have to think of all the ways people can hack into or compromise the system or process in order to develop something that is secure enough. Inevitably it isn't the technology that creates an opportunity for fraud; it is the people using it. Identity management is also the latest hot topic in the consulting world, which means that to be considered an expert in the field you only have to know slightly more than nothing. What better qualifications do I need to write a book about it? It is also something that will most likely excite my organisation enough for them to allow me to take time off to write a book about it. Or so I think.

I read my organisation's corporate policy on working part-time. It seems to be easy. All I have to do is fill in a form and send it off to the HR department for approval. HR will then speak to my manager and come back to me with a response within a week. I download the application form, and that's when the trouble begins.

I have to tick which part-time work option I am applying for. The options are 'parental leave', 'carer's leave' or 'study leave'. That is it. There isn't a box on the form for writer's leave. There isn't even a box for 'other'.

I phone Garry my boss and tell him straight out that I want to work part-time. He says, 'Are you pregnant?' I say, 'No.' He says, 'I don't understand.'

I explain that I want time off to write a book. Garry laughs and says that I can't just work part-time simply because I want to. He says he can't set that sort of precedent in the organisation. If he lets me work part-time, everybody might want to do it.

I am outraged. If I had a child I wouldn't have to ask for permission. It would just be a matter of filling in a form. I ask Garry what difference it makes if I want to take time off to look after a baby or write a book. Surely the net effect to him and the organisation is exactly the same. He says it is all about commitment.

He is right to question my commitment, but that isn't the point; surely it shouldn't be a natural assumption simply because I want to work part-time. It seems bizarre to conclude that having other interests in my life means that I am less committed to my job. Surely people can have equal commitment to both?

But it isn't about commitment; it is about the law. Unlike the parents of real babies, there are no laws protecting the rights of people with metaphorical babies.

Last year, my friend Jules applied for three months' leave because she wanted to go travelling. She applied for the leave nine months in advance. Her organisation immediately said no. When she pursued the matter, she was told that she needed to write an essay explaining what she would be doing during her time off and how it would benefit the organisation. Essentially she was asked to justify how she would spend her private time: time when she was not working and not being paid.

Despite all the talk from management and HR departments about work–life balance, the whole concept is bullshit. Companies don't want us to be balanced and well-rounded individuals. And why would they? They want us to devote our whole lives and link our entire identities to our jobs. It's only then that they get 60 hours a week out of us for the price of 40. The flip side of this is how poorly working mothers would fare if they weren't protected by the law. Based on the debate I am having with my boss, I wonder if companies would grant part-time work to working mothers if they weren't obligated. It's tragic to think how little progress we have made as a society.

I am not prepared to take no for an answer from Garry, so I quickly change the focus of my argument. I explain that the book I want to write is about identity management, which will not only build my personal brand as a consultant in the field, it will also be great publicity for the organisation.

It works. I pique his interest. He supports the idea and even commends me for my initiative. But instead of allowing me to work part-time, Garry says he will reduce my consulting load to three or four days a week, thus giving me time to write the book. This way he isn't creating the precedent of allowing people to work part-time.

For a moment, I think I am about to have my cake and eat it too. Here I am being allowed to write a book and being paid to write it. I won't have to live on a part-time income after all. Then comes the catch.

In return for allowing me to write, my company will have editorial control of the content of the book, the book will be co-branded with the organisation's name and logo, and the organisation will keep the royalties.

I realise that this cake is coated in marzipan. It looks great, but it leaves a bitter taste in my mouth.

I'm not prepared to surrender editorial control of the book. I can see the book turning into a promotional brochure for my organisation. It won't be my baby; it will end up as just another consulting assignment. I realise that I need more than just an opportunity to write; I also need autonomy. I want to have some freedom in my life to do my own thing. And two days of freedom and autonomy are more important to me than two days of income.

I thank Garry for his generous offer but say that if it is all the same to him I'd prefer not to be paid to write the book, not to co-brand and not to share the royalties. As it turns out, it is not all the same to him.

Garry's counter-argument starts off friendly. He tells me that he'd like to help me win the company's Thought Leadership Award for my book, but I need to abide by his conditions to do so. I almost laugh. Are we back in school? As if I'd trade my intellectual property for the grown-up equivalent of a gold star. When I still refuse to cooperate, his Mr Nice-guy act dries up, and he tells me to read my contract – the organisation owns everything I write anyway, even if I write it in my own time.

The bullying tactics make me even more determined not to give in. And given that Garry is still negotiating with me rather than shutting the conversation down and telling me to get back to work, I realise that he thinks the book is a good idea. If he cares so much about my idea, he must think it could be valuable. And if it is valuable, I'm certainly not going to share it with him.

After several weeks of discussion, the final word is that I can take one day a week off without pay for six months to write the book. I will maintain full editorial control over the content of the book, but it will be branded with the corporate colours and logo, and the company will own the intellectual property (and therefore the royalties) when it is finished. It is akin to granting maternity leave as long as the organisation owns the baby at the end of it and can tattoo the corporate logo on its butt.

I hate that an organisation will have a claim over what I do in my own time, but I agree to the terms because I am so desperate to have a day off every week.

Chris and my friends are so supportive of my decision to take time off to write. Jules says, 'Well, it's about time. You're such a good writer. I can't believe it's taken you so long to do it.' I love my friends.

The only problem is, I don't write – not a single word. Every Friday, I wake up and cheer that I don't have to go to work. Then I go to a café for breakfast, take Toffee to the park, read a book (about anything other than identity management) and then go back to a café again.

After a few weeks, Chris challenges me on how I am spending my Fridays. I realise that I'm not writing anything because I don't want my bastard organisation to own it. But that is only part of the problem. Regardless of ownership, who in their right mind would choose to spend one day a week writing about identity management without being paid for it? What was I thinking? Writing about identity management isn't fun or creative. Just because I know something about the subject doesn't mean I should spend my time writing about it. I think back to Madam Barbara, who told me that I needed to help people through my writing. I am hardly going to change people's lives with a topic like that. If this is my metaphorical baby, it would be dead from neglect.

Chris points out that I have two problems to solve – sorting out the intellectual property ownership impediment and finding something interesting to write about.

30

ALL BY HERSELF

'I've worked it out,' Emma announces. 'I've worked out what I'm going to do with my life.'

Chris and I are having brunch with Emma at our favourite café. I am surprised when she walks, or should I say bounces, into the café. I haven't seen her this excited since she was crowned as the local pub karaoke champion for singing 'Stairway to Heaven'. Despite Emma's perfectly accessorised exterior, she is just as common as the rest of us on the inside.

'I need to work for myself,' she says.

'Of course you do,' Chris says. 'I've been telling you that for months.'

After visiting Madam Barbara the clairvoyant, Emma thought long and hard about what she could do in order to work for herself. Emma's independence is a blessing and a curse for her – her independence drives her to want to work for herself, but it also makes it more risky. Because of her independence she doesn't have anybody to support her or to fall back on if things don't work out. If she weren't so independent, she'd probably be married and more financially secure, which would make it easier to take the risk of leaving the security of an employer and going out on her own.

Madam Barbara's prediction has inspired Emma to think about her options relentlessly until she has come up with a way to make it work.

Chris can't believe what he is hearing. 'Are you telling me that you needed a clairvoyant to tell you this? As if some strange woman with a crystal ball knows you better than your own friends?'

The clairvoyant has given Emma confidence. She had already worked out that she wanted to work for herself, but Madam Barbara's prediction has validated her idea and helped her believe that she can actually do it.

Emma had decided years ago that she would one day own her own business. She'd been inspired by her boss at her very first job – the sexist pig who said he only hired her because he couldn't find a boy. 'He was a complete idiot, and he ran a successful business despite himself,' she says. 'At the time I thought, "If he can make a business work, then surely I can."'

She's also seen how much happier her father became when he transitioned from employee to self-employed. She's witnessed both the lifestyle and financial rewards he's received from taking the risk, and her father has always said that he wished he'd done it ten years earlier.

Over the last few months, Emma has been thinking about different ways of finding her give-a-shit again, without success. She has considered finding a less stressful job or doing something that is more community-minded, but it just didn't seem the right thing to do. She's come to the conclusion that, despite her discontent, she does in fact enjoy the profession of marketing, so a complete career change won't solve the problem, nor will a flat move to another company. Emma has already tried changing jobs and that didn't fix anything. In the end, she keeps coming back to autonomy. 'When you combine knowing that people like us are highly capable, with my desire for autonomy, then working for myself is a really logical thing to do.'

And how is she going to do it? How is she going to own her own business and minimise the risk enough so she can sleep at night?

Emma has decided to conduct a management buyout of the sub-business she is managing at the telecommunications company. The sub-business doesn't fit naturally with the rest of the company, and to solve this problem in other countries they have simply sold the businesses off. Emma feels confident that she can convince the people at the top to do the same with her business.

'It ticks all the boxes,' Emma says. 'I'll be doing something for myself, but it also appeals to my conservative side because it is essentially the same as what I'm doing now, so it's less risky.'

'Let me get this straight,' I say. 'You're going to buy the same business that you are managing now to do the same thing as you have been doing all these months that you've been miserable, and you'll carry the financial risk?'

'Yes. But it'll be mine,' Emma says. 'I won't have to put up with any management bullshit. And it will be my decision how much it becomes my identity. If I make my work my life, it's my choice and my expectations.'

I don't really see the attraction, but it doesn't matter. Nor does it matter if Emma's decision has been influenced by an old woman with a crystal ball or anybody else. The transformation in Emma is undeniable and almost unbelievable. She is energised and enthusiastic, and she cares about her work again. She isn't tired or grumpy any more. While she is waiting for management to make a decision about the sale, she starts treating the business as if it is hers already. Her wandering days are over, and she stops stealing time and going to cafés and parks. After a full day's work, Emma stays back in the office for hours working on business plans and predictive financial analysis for her new business. In her mind, she is already banking her millions and has decided she'll work 10 a.m. to 7 p.m. because she's not a morning person.

Emma has found her baby.

31

BRAVE NEW WORLD

'To a brave new world,' toasts one of our managers as he lifts his glass of French champagne. Apparently he hasn't read the book, or, if he has, he didn't understand that it is about a dystopia. This guy has never struck me as much of a reader.

All the employees at my company have been summoned to an urgent meeting in the boardroom to listen to an announcement from a couple of suits from head office over a speaker phone. The expensive bubbly – the type I only drink when somebody else is paying – is thrust into our hands, and we are all commanded to toast. The only problem is it doesn't feel much like a celebration. If the champagne weren't so expensive I would put it down in disgust.

The tinny voices on the speaker phone have just announced that they are selling off our local organisation to another company – one that does not have the prestigious brand, big clients, big budgets and multinational reach of our existing organisation. Despite the corporate spin and the flashy PowerPoint slides, everyone in the room knows that we are screwed. We've been sold off to a second-rate company and everything is about to change. The lucky ones will be forced to sign new contracts, and the unlucky ones will be out of a job.

I look across the boardroom table at the stunned faces of my colleagues, all with glasses of champagne resting awkwardly in their hands. Some of these people have been with the organisation their entire careers. It seems surreal that we've been effectively cut loose, absolved of any obligation, via a teleconference that lasted about ten minutes.

Margaret, the administration manager who's served the company for 30 years, is visibly distressed, yet her feelings seem to go unnoticed by the head of the acquiring company as he tells us what an exciting opportunity this is for all involved and how they really care about their employees. Margaret's sole responsibility is to enter data into the proprietary management software system. She is an expert on the system, but there will be no need for her skills at the new company, and at her age it is unlikely anybody will invest in retraining her. She is fucked, and everybody in the room knows it, despite the attempt to pretend otherwise.

This episode unfolding before me in the boardroom reminds me of an interview I saw on television with the Slovenian philosopher Slavoj Žižek about the difference between traditional authoritarian power and post-modern totalitarianism. Žižek tells a story about a child who is asked to visit his grandmother. An old-fashioned authoritarian father would say, 'I don't care how you feel, just go there and behave properly.' A post-modern permissive totalitarian father will tell the child that he only has to go if he wants to but will then say to him, 'But you know how much your grandmother would love to see you.' Beneath the appearance of this free choice there is an even more oppressive order. Not only does the child have to visit his grandmother, he also has to like it. The freedom to sulk has been removed. Like the child in Žižek's story, not only are we being turfed out by our organisation, we are being commanded to celebrate it.

I have no intention of participating in the farcical celebration and make no attempt to disguise my disgust. I attract the attention of the head of HR, who hurries down to the other end of the table to speak to me. He showers me with flattery and praise. Apparently I am fiercely ambitious, highly committed and very intelligent – just the sort of person they need for their 'brave new world'. Ambitious and committed? Me? That goes to show how in tune Human Resources is with their human resources.

Even though the HR director's patronising remarks rile me, I know that I am one of the lucky ones in the room. What has been sold here is people and intellectual property, and my education and skills are in high demand in the market at the moment. They need to make sure that people like me don't leave, because it will reduce the value of the sale. Although in six months' time, if market demand swings in a different direction, I daresay I wouldn't be considered to be nearly so committed or intelligent.

Just weeks earlier, three senior employees were sacked with immediate effect, reportedly without a penny of compensation. In the case of one valuable employee, the axe had fallen so swiftly that the client phoned the office the next day to ask his whereabouts. In the phone hook-up announcing their departure, management assured us that this wasn't personal and that this didn't mean they weren't good people. Apparently they just hadn't met their targets.

Despite my relative security and the fact that I have lost my give-a-shit anyway, I am surprisingly unsettled by the announcement. This new organisation is not what I signed up for when I joined the company. They've changed the rules partway through the game, and, childish as it may seem, I feel hurt and betrayed.

So I do what any self-respecting girl would do. I swipe a bottle of champagne and go to visit my best friend.

Emma also has some bad news. Her company has refused her offer to buy out her business. 'It would have been so easy and so good,' she says.

'What are you going to do now?' I ask.

'Fuck knows.'

32

REVERSE DISCRIMINATION

As luck would have it, Annabel the headhunter phones the next day to tell me that Company ABC would like to make me an offer to join them as senior change management consultant. It has been so long since the interview that I'd almost forgotten all about it. Getting a job offer feels so good. I feel validated and wanted. And a new job will give me a break from the monotony and boredom of the daily grind. Any new job is interesting for the first few months because of the learning curve. But I have a good feeling about this job. I like the vision and passion of the manager. Maybe this job could sustain my interest.

But then I remember that regardless of how good the job might be, I only want to do it part-time. I've made a commitment to write, and I am determined to stick to it. I tell Annabel that I am thrilled to hear the news and would love to join the organisation, but my situation has changed and I am now only able to work three days a week. Annabel says, 'I didn't think you had children.'

I explain my position and then she explains hers. She says that ABC Company has never employed anybody on a part-time basis before, so she isn't going to waste their time by asking them to consider it in my case. She gives me an ultimatum – either I accept the job on a full-time basis or she will tell them that I have withdrawn my application. I tell her that I am only prepared to work part-time.

I am really pissed off when I hang up the phone from Annabel, verging on militant. If I am good enough to be employed five days a week, why wouldn't I be good enough to be employed three days? Surely the qualities that inspired my decision to write a book – such as initiative, courage and creativity – should be celebrated and valued? But Annabel isn't even prepared to ask Company ABC if they'd consider me part-time. I feel like she is betraying me and the sisterhood by perpetuating the patriarchal and restrictive definition of work. Why should we always conform to the male structure and conventions of work when it clearly makes so many women miserable? Must we forever be unhappy participants in a man's world?

I'm not prepared to give up without a fight. Company ABC should at least be told the truth about my situation rather than just being told that I've withdrawn my application. I send an email to the consultant who conducted my second interview at Company ABC and explain the situation. I hear nothing back from him, but at least I feel better that he now knows the truth.

I start making a serious effort with the job hunt. I am lucky that there seems to be a shortage in the market of people with my skills. Consequently I am invited to an interview for every job I apply for. And once my CV is circulating, the headhunters start to swarm. I am getting two or three calls from headhunters every week. It is intoxicating to feel so wanted. For the first time in my working life, I feel like I have the power in the employee–employer relationship – that is until I mention the 'P' word.

The discussion with recruiters is always the same. They start off flattering me, saying that I can practically name my price. Then I tell them I want to work three days a week. They look disappointed and ask me if I have children, telling me that it will be harder to find a job, but in a booming market like this it is still possible. Once I tell them I don't have children, that I just want to work part-time to pursue other interests, they hastily usher me out of their office as if I am wasting their time. I consider lying and just telling them that I have kids, but I can't do it. I feel like I would be dishonouring working mothers and betraying all the other 30-something and over it women who might also want to work part-time for no other reason than because they can. In a bizarre way, I feel like a trailblazer – a modern-day suffragette.

I ring Emma to bitch and moan about the injustice thrust upon childless women. She suggests we medicate our disappointment with cocktails and a beach holiday. I'm sure that's what the suffragettes would have wanted us to do!

33

THE END OF THE WORLD
AS WE KNOW IT

Emma and I are on a boat bound for a coral reef when the brave new world collapses.

Work is the furthest thing from my mind when a colleague phones to say that the sale of our local office has fallen through. There had just been another urgent all-staff phone hook-up, but this time there was no French champagne. Things turned bad during the due diligence, and the purchasing company has withdrawn its offer.

What this means for the future of my organisation and my job is unknown at this stage. Apparently all will be revealed in another all-staff phone hook-up later that evening.

Trying not to focus on my potential retrenchment and mortgage payments, Emma and I spend the day dressed head-to-toe in hired faded-blue Lycra bodysuits to protect us from the sun and the stingers while we snorkel over coral. Just how many people have worn this figure-hugging suit before me doesn't bear thinking about.

The reef is amazing. Some of the coral is over 800 years old, although, just like the Lycra bodysuits, it isn't as brightly coloured and pristine looking as in the brochure. 'Coral is just like people,' the marine biologist tells us. 'Ten per cent of it is really beautiful, and the rest is plain. It's only the beautiful 10 per cent that gets its photo taken for magazines.'

The turtles are the highlight: big beautiful things floating around and getting high on sea grass. I tell one of the turtles I am about to lose my job, and he looks at me as if to say, 'Chill out, man.' Turtles don't get worked up about anything. It takes 50 years before they reach their sexual maturity. If that was me, I reckon I'd be looking a little more agitated.

The boat is delayed coming back from the reef, so I am 20 minutes late dialling into the all-staff phone hook-up. I only catch the tail end of the announcement where the suits in head office are telling us that no decisions have been made about our future yet and we should just continue adding value for our clients as best we can for the next 48 hours. By then they will have considered all the options and will get back to us with a decision about the future of the organisation.

I sit on the balcony of our hotel room sipping a margarita and listening to my colleagues back in the office ask futile questions of the management. Some of my colleagues sound angry and aggressive, others are still hopeful. The worst part of all is listening to one of the hot-shot consultants who sounds stunned and shell-shocked. His usual bravado has been replaced by a tone of desperation – a helpless man staring into the face of unemployment and unmet mortgage payments. It is almost unbearable to listen to him. Another consultant starts ranting about how the situation isn't good enough and that after all our years of dedicated service we deserve to be treated with more respect.

Emma presses the mute button on the phone and says, 'Your colleagues are so naive. The executives are all talking bullshit anyway. They don't give a crap about any of you. You're all just a problem they need to get rid of before you all become destructive.'

She is right. We are all about to be discarded and forgotten: just like those poor bastards they sacked a couple of weeks ago for not meeting their targets. What were their names again?

The executives try to calm everybody down by telling us they will work day and night to assess all the options. When things get really heated, one of the consultants says that they are talking to another potential buyer, but for commercial reasons he can't disclose any of the details at this time. To me, it sounds like a lie; he is just trying to appease everybody. But Garry doesn't interpret it that way.

'You mean to say that there is another party involved and you haven't informed me about it?' Garry bellows into the phone. 'As the head of this organisation I find it unacceptable.' I can hear the fury in his voice, and I start to feel sorry for him. 'I have been working day and night for the good of everyone on this call and to find out that you have been working behind my back is totally unacceptable.' I hear the slamming of a fist on a desk and a shuffling of chairs, and the call is quickly brought to a close. All we can do now is wait – and continue to add value to our clients, of course.

In the early days of my career, I viewed my relationship to the company I worked for as familial. I was loyal and trusting, and in return they would be loyal to me. I believed them when they said I was valued, and I did stupid things like work every weekend and toss and turn at night worrying about deadlines. I even delayed my European working-holiday plans, at great inconvenience to my boyfriend at the time who had already resigned from his job, because my company 'needed' me to stay until the end of the project.

I'm a lot more cynical and jaded now, and consequently am not at all surprised by the way management is treating us. But some of my colleagues have spent their whole careers at this organisation, joining as graduates and slowly and steadily climbing the corporate ladder through dutiful service. I fear that some of them still believed in the 'corporate family' fantasy. Poor bastards. Imagine devoting yourself to an organisation for your whole career, only to find out you are just a pawn in a transaction and that no matter what you have accomplished, what you have sacrificed and how diligently you have served, you can be discarded just as easily as the next person. It is prostitution with your clothes on.

One IT consulting company has dispensed with the pretence that they value their staff as individuals and refers to them as 'tokens' rather than 'employees'. I was horrified when I first heard this. Now I give them credit for being honest and upfront.

The first time I realised that companies don't care about their staff was when I was all alone in a dirty, dingy Chinese hospital. I was working for a government department at the time and was in Hong Kong for a conference when I contracted acute food poisoning. On the second day of the conference, I went back to my hotel room because I was feeling a bit queasy. I thought that if I lay down for a couple of hours and had a cup of tea I'd be OK. About ten minutes later, I started vomiting, and then kept on vomiting and kept on vomiting. I got my pillow and settled in next to the toilet for the evening. At the time, I had no idea about the seriousness of my condition. It hadn't occurred to me that I should tell somebody or even that I might need medical attention.

A few hours later, my boss came to my hotel room to borrow a power converter. I tried to stand up but couldn't, so I crawled to the door to let her in. And that's all I remember until I woke up in a hospital bed staring up at a woman standing above me with crazy eyes and a scalpel in her hand. She was screaming at me in Chinese and waving the sharp, pointy blade at me. Two people in white coats rushed over, tackled her to the ground, put a straitjacket on her and took her away.

I was left lying there by myself wondering what the hell was going on. I sat up and looked around me. It was dark, but I could see that I was sharing a ward with two Chinese men – and I swear both of them looked like they were two hundred years old. Talk about heaven's waiting room.

There was nobody else around, so I called out. Nothing. I called again. Nobody came. By this stage I was freaking out, so I got out of bed to investigate. I only made it a couple of steps before I fainted from what I was later to find out was low blood pressure. When I regained consciousness, I tried to get up off the floor but couldn't. I called out for help but again nobody came, so I curled up on the floor and cried until eventually I saw a patient wandering along the hall.

She was talking to herself and wringing her hands. I knew she was loopy, but she appeared to be my only option at that point in time. I pointed to my empty bed and raised my hands up signalling for her to help me. We staggered back to the bed, and she stood there watching me as I got settled into the sheets. Then she reached out and gently touched a tear running down my face. She turned around and walked away, resuming the conversation she had been having with herself.

I must have fallen asleep, because the next thing I knew it was daylight and my boss was staring down at me with a concerned expression on her face. She'd brought a familiar face along with her. Ashley was the flatmate of my boyfriend at the time and was also attending the conference. They told me that I had been rushed to the nearest hospital, which happened to be a charity hospital. It was dark, dingy, poor and run-down. To make matters worse, the only spare bed in the hospital was in the psych ward. They promised that they would speak to our colleagues at the embassy and get me moved to a better hospital immediately. In the meantime, I was to rest until my blood pressure returned to normal levels. The doctor assured me this would only take 24 hours. Twenty-four hours stretched into forty-eight, which stretched into seventy-two and so on. Three days later, I was still in the shithole of a hospital. My colleagues came to visit me every day, and every day they apologised for not having moved me to a better hospital yet. The problem was that the executive general manager was in town and everybody was so busy looking after him they didn't have time to help me. On the fourth day, the conference ended and everyone returned home except for Ashley, who said she'd stay with me to make sure I was OK. I was in that hideous hospital for six days in total. In that time, I'd watched both of the men next to me die, mastered the bedpan and got an infection from what was believed to be a dirty needle.

There was still no sign of anybody from the embassy, so when it came time to check out of the hospital I was handed a bill and told they wouldn't give me back my passport until I paid it. Ashley and I traipsed around the backstreets of Hong Kong looking for a cash machine. I was still fragile and wobbly on my feet, and I had to max out both Ashley's and my credit cards to pay the bill. To this day, I am so grateful to Ashley for staying behind with me.

The infection from the dirty needle was cleared up by a dose of antibiotics, but it could have been much worse. Essentially my organisation put me in, and kept me in, a life-threatening situation and was too busy wining and dining the executive general manager to visit me in hospital, move me to another, or even to pay the bill.

This experience taught me two lessons: that no matter how much I love the company I work for, it will never love me back, and to drink whisky with every meal while travelling to prevent food poisoning. I've applied this strategy on every overseas trip since and haven't once got sick. I highly recommend it.

34

FINDING MY GIVE-A-SHIT

At the teleconference 48 hours later, there is still no news. Apparently the managers from head office are still considering all the options and they will get back to us in another 48 hours. Somebody on the call asks for a definitive timeline for when they will make their decisions and communicate with staff. The pompous suit from head office chairing the call says that he has plans for his wife's birthday next week so he intends to have everything sorted by then.

What an asshole. People are staring down the barrel of defaulting on their mortgage payments and this guy is more concerned with his wife's birthday. I am astounded by his lack of empathy. I know I shouldn't be surprised by it, but it is still shocking to hear.

Some of my colleagues are holding out hope that another buyer will be found and our jobs will be safe. In my gut, I am sure that there isn't another buyer. The only thing being bought right now is time. Management is just buying time to plan their public announcement and arrange the redundancy details. So I start preparing for the worst.

As I am sorting out my files and saving a copy of my business contacts, Annabel the headhunter phones. Company ABC has changed their employment policy and has decided to offer me the job on a part-time basis. They will allow me to work three days a week for six months. After half a year, they will review the arrangement to see if it is working. Annabel says, 'You must have really impressed them, because you will be the first person they have ever employed on a part-time basis.'

When I speak to the HR manager from Company ABC to accept the offer, he congratulates me for setting a precedent for flexible employment. Women who were previously working full-time were allowed to work part-time when they returned from maternity leave, but I am the first person they have employed on a part-time basis from the outset.

I am proud of myself. I have changed organisational policy and set a precedent in a multinational company. I feel like I've just scored a goal for the sisterhood. And that's when I realise how I can help people through my writing. I can write about being 30-something and over it.

I am still thinking about my writing plans when the axe falls. I was right: there was no alternative buyer. It seems management needed the extra time to work out how to pay as little as possible in redundancies. Not only is the financial compensation mean and stingy, so too is the way in which the shutdown is handled. The managers are so clinical; they convey no empathy, no regret and no compassion. It is the most unceremonious occasion I have ever experienced. I feel sick to the core when I overhear one manager say, 'It's not personal, it's business.' I understand that businesses have to make hard decisions, but how can he possibly not understand that the consequences of his business decision are very personal indeed? I wonder how he can sleep at night.

I have my fair share of sleepless nights. I feel too guilty to sleep – guilty that everyone else's lives are in turmoil when mine is looking the best it has in ages. I can't believe how lucky I am to be able to work three days a week for a company that seems interesting, and two days on writing something that matters to me.

I am unemployed for one day and then I start my new job at Company ABC. In my first week, my boss takes me out to lunch to welcome me to the company. He asks me about my writing, and

I tell him I think it will take me more than six months to write the book. To my amazement and delight he says that if I want to continue working part-time after the six-month period he will support it. 'The most important thing to me is that you're happy. Because if you're happy, then you'll work better,' he says.

And you know what? He is right.

All of a sudden, I don't resent going to work any more. I'm not over it any more. Partly it is because I am still in the honeymoon period of a new job, but most of all it is because I've found *it*. I've found what I've been searching for for almost a year. I've found my give-a-shit.

And, amazingly, Emma has, too.

It takes me a while to notice – partly because I am focused on the changes going on in my life but also because I'm not expecting it. But one day I realise that Emma isn't pissed off any more. She is calm and settled, and instead of calling me to bitch about how much she hates work, she is talking about work as if it interests her, as if she cares about it.

I ask her one morning over coffee, 'Have you become contented in your discontent?'

She thinks about it for a while and says, 'Now that I think about it, I'm not discontented any more.'

Even though Emma is disappointed that her management buyout has fallen through, she's realised that she is still able to get excited about work. 'I thought I'd lost that excitement for ever,' she says. 'But when I was planning the buyout, it came back and it felt great.'

Knowing that her enthusiasm for work was not lost for ever is enough for her to snap out of her funk and to stop thinking that everything about work is shit. She doesn't love work the way she used to in her 20s, but she can tolerate all the things she doesn't like because she has something to look forward to now and something to work towards – her next opportunity to own her own business.

Emma doesn't know when the next opportunity will arrive or what it will be, but she's decided to keep doing what she is doing until the opportunity comes along. 'I'm not frustrated waiting for the next opportunity,' she says, 'because I'm using this time to prepare for it.' Emma is focusing on her savings so she'll have more money to invest next time around, and she is concentrating on learning as much about running a business as she can.

'I know what I want to do now, but I don't want to do it half-arsed,' she says. 'I'm prepared to be patient, and in the meantime I'll sponge off my current job for all I can. I can reconcile that with the knowledge that I'm just a commodity at work. Now I view work as something I can use to my advantage. I can make my dumb mistakes on someone else's money.' Emma has even put her hand up for a promotion so she can get more experience.

It occurs to me that despite Emma's newfound optimism, nothing in her day-to-day life has changed. She still goes to the same office, does the same work and puts up with the same dickheads. Somehow, though, everything is different. Once Emma worked out what she wants and feels like she is en route to achieving it she is happy again. The fact that she hasn't achieved it yet doesn't seem to matter. 'Maybe knowing what you want to do is 90 per cent of the answer,' Emma says. 'Clarity about what I want brings peace of mind, and that seems to be enough.'

Emma made a choice about her next path in life and by doing so she added a few more boxes that haven't been ticked yet. And that made all the difference.

35

MY BABY

I have found my elusive baby – something to think about, care about and nurture. And it is the best feeling in the world.

It doesn't take long to adjust to my part-time income. In fact, I can honestly say that after a couple of months I don't even notice any more. Susan Maushart refers to gender role research in *What Women Want Next* that shows that not only do women earn less money than men, they are often also satisfied with less. I don't know if it is a female thing or just a matter of getting used to it, but I have adjusted so fully to my new spending pattern that I don't feel like I am going without. Maushart wrote: 'The main positive life events that contribute to a sense of genuine well-being are almost ridiculously achievable on any budget: the basic pleasures of food, drink, sleep and sex; and relationships with friends.' She is right. I still feel like I have enough money to buy everything I need and want, *and* I have two days a week to write. It feels like a fairy tale – three days a week to enrich my wallet and two days to enrich my soul. I can hardly believe I've pulled it off.

My friend Troy, who is the master of back-handed compliments, says, 'It's amazing how you managed to get your shit together like this. When I first met you, you were a mess. Now you're on top of the world.'

One day on the way to work I suddenly realise that I'm not bored any more – not even at work. I no longer hope for a bomb-threat or that legionnaires' disease will be discovered in the air-conditioning ducts so I can go home. I don't hate going to work any more. But more than that, I realise that work adds something important to my life.

As an extrovert, I need the things that work provides me with. I need the connection and feedback of working in a team, the security of a regular income and the structure of a working day.

Don't get me wrong: I don't love work – not in the way I used to in my 20s. But I don't need to any more in order to be happy, and that's a big change for me. Like Rodney the consultant with the concentric circles, there are other things in my life now that enrich me, so my expectations of what work will give me have lowered. Work is just one ingredient in my fulfilled and happy life. I need work to be able to enjoy writing, and I need writing to be able to enjoy work.

When one of my former clients – the porn lover with the penchant for discipline – phones to offer me a job in his new company, I feel like I am being tested. He promises me a fast-track career path and says that in three years' time I could be promoted to partner and earning £400,000 a year, but I'll have to work full-time. I hear the words 'promotion' and 'more money' and feel my dormant flame of ambition ignite again. It is like an involuntary reflex. I guess there is no hiding from the years of conditioning. But then I think, 'Why?' Why would I want a promotion? Why would I want more money? Why would I throw away my new-found balance, happiness and creativity? Have I learned nothing over the last 12 months?

I say thanks but no thanks, and he says I am crazy. 'You won't make that sort of money writing books,' he says. I tell him I am writing for love, not money, and he laughs and says, 'The Kasey Edwards I know doesn't do anything if it's not for money. Think about it, babe, you could buy a lot of lingerie with £400,000.'

The guy is a creepy, misogynist fuckwit, and I don't believe for a moment I could be earning that sort of money in three years' time. But none of that matters anyway. My life is the richest I've ever known.

36

THE ANSWER

I hate chapters like this – chapters that claim to list the magic formulae – solving all your problems in ten easy steps. But what I hate more than books with final chapters like this is books without final chapters like this. If you're anything like me, you would have flicked to this chapter just after you read the introduction, or maybe even halfway through. I can't tell you how many final chapters of self-help books I have flicked to in the hope of finding 'The Answer'. But it wasn't until I finished writing my own book that I realised that 'The Answer' is not something you can read in a book, hear from a guru or swallow in a pill, and as long as you keep looking for something like that it will always be lost.

I'm about to write the worst cliché ever written. Looking back over the last 12 months of my life and considering all the things that I've learned in the process of losing my give-a-shit and finding it again, this cliché seems to sum it up. Get ready, here it comes . . . the answer is the *journey*.

Yuck. I can't believe I just wrote that. If you haven't shut the book in disgust, let me try to explain. I needed to be discontented and frustrated until it became unbearable. In consulting, we talk about people needing a compelling reason to change. We use a Bunsen burner analogy, saying that when the flame is burning yellow people aren't distressed enough to change. We need to wait until the flame

217

turns to blue or white before things really start happening. I needed to be so over being over it and so fucked up before I was able to fight my way out of it.

This point is more elegantly illustrated in the story about the girl and the butterfly. It goes like this. A girl watched a butterfly trying to break free from its cocoon. She could see the butterfly was struggling against the constraints of the silk. It seemed to make progress by pushing part of its wing out of the cocoon, but then it would flop back inside again. The girl wanted to help the butterfly, so she got some scissors and cut the cocoon. The butterfly tumbled out of the cocoon and landed on the ground. And that's where it lay. It tried to spread its wings, but it couldn't. It was stuck there on the ground immobilised, and that's where it stayed and that's where it died.

Getting out of the cocoon is hard work for butterflies and it takes time. But the process of fighting against the constraints of the silk is necessary for them to learn to use their wings. Without the struggle, their own personal struggle in their own time, they will never be able to fly.

It took me almost a year to fight my way out of the cocoon. The strange thing is that in the first couple of months of looking I was given the answer. My friend Godfrey told me I needed a baby and that baby was writing. He was right, but I needed many more months of discovery, reflection and budgeting before I was ready to take his advice. The answer had to come from within me.

When I asked Caroline the life coach what advice she would give people in my situation, she said, 'You know better than that, Kasey. It's not for me to give advice. All the knowledge required already resides within each person. Sometimes they just need somebody to shine a flashlight into the darkness so they can see it.'

Just as nobody else could cut my cocoon for me, I would not presume to try to cut anybody else's. The best I can hope for is that my story might be a flashlight or a glimmer of hope for somebody else who is 30-something and over it.

Emma and I started our stories in the same place, yet our journeys were different and so were our answers. But along the way we took comfort and inspiration from the wisdom of other people and the support of each other. So in keeping with the format, I have prepared a list of ten things I learned over the last year that may inspire you.

1. Putting all of our happiness eggs into the career basket is asking for trouble. People who are happiest with their jobs are either not thinking about what they are doing and why, or they have the lowest expectations about what work will bring to their lives. John Stuart Mill in his book *Utilitarianism* said that it was important 'not to expect more from life than it is capable of bestowing'. The same applies to our jobs. A job will never fulfil our relationship needs, it's unlikely to link us to our communities and if it is a source of friendship we need to be clear about the distinction between friendship and networking associates. Meaning and fulfilment can come from many areas of our life. Work is just one ingredient in a happy life.

2. Trading in relationships, hobbies and authenticity for a high-paying, high-status and high-stress job is the fastest way to misery.

3. Working may not be the express route to happiness, but not working seems to be the fast track to unhappiness. Fun and freedom are not enough to sustain us. Rather than fantasising about not working, it's more productive to spend our time finding something to do that is meaningful.

4. We all need a baby. We need something to care about that is bigger than ourselves – something to nurture, grow and invest in.

5. It's not too late to change our path. The people who genuinely believe that life is full of opportunities are much happier about their jobs than those who don't. We don't have to look for a job or a career for life. Just find something that brings us happiness now.

6. We don't have to turn our backs on all the skills we've developed and experience we've had simply because we are unhappy at work. We should work out which things we can keep and transfer into something new.

7. We shouldn't delay making changes to our lives because we're waiting for the best option to come along. Sometimes any sort of action is better than nothing.

8. Once we've been unplugged from the matrix, it's almost impossible to plug ourselves back in. If you're 30-something and over it, it's not going to go away. Use this crisis to propel yourself into finding your own answers and your own happiness.

9. You'll know that you've found your give-a-shit when you are energised and optimistic. You'll work hard, but it won't feel like hard work. Don't expect to find it straight away; the journey takes time. And once you find it, don't expect it to last for ever. As I learned from meditating, everything in life is impermanent, so enjoy things while they last and then move on.

10. While being 30-something and over it feels like shit, it's a really positive milestone in our lives. It forces us to pause, take a breath and ask ourselves what's important to us and what we want out of life. It's like a safety valve to stop us from getting to old age and wondering what the hell we did that for. Like my brother Michael said, sometimes we just need to be whipped.

SUGGESTIONS FOR FURTHER READING

Bolles, Richard N., *What Color is Your Parachute?* (Ten Speed Press, 2006)

Bronson, Po, *What Should I Do With My Life?* (Vintage, 2004)

Byrne, Rhonda, *The Secret* (Simon & Schuster, 2006)

Fallick, Kaye, *Get a New Life: How to Change the Way You Live* (Allen & Unwin, 2004)

Frankel, Lois, *Nice Girls Don't Get The Corner Office: 101 Unconscious Mistakes Women Make* (Business Plus Imports, 2005)

Frankl, Viktor, *Man's Search for Meaning* (Rider & Co, 2004)

Gilbert, Elizabeth, *Eat Pray Love: One Woman's Search for Everything* (Bloomsbury Publishing, 2007)

Haussegger, Virginia, *Wonder Woman: The Myth of Having It All* (Allen & Unwin, 2005)

James, Oliver, *Affluenza* (Vermilion, 2007)

Lewis, Gwyneth, *Sunbathing in the Rain: A Cheerful Book About Depression* (HarperPerennial, 2006)

Marsh, Nigel *Fat, Forty and Fired* (Piatkus Books, 2006)

Marsh, Nigel, *Observations of a Very Short Man* (Allen & Unwin, 2007)

Maushart, Susan, *What Women Want Next* (Bloomsbury, 2007)

Mill, John Stuart, *Utilitarianism* (Hackett Publishing, 2002)

Pinker, Susan, *The Sexual Paradox* (Atlantic Books, 2008)

Redfield, James, *Celestine Prophecy* (Bantam Books, 1994)

Schwartz, Barry, *The Paradox of Choice: Why More is Less* (HarperCollins, 2005)

Sher, Barbara, *I Could Do Anything, If Only I Knew What It Was* (Bantam Doubleday Dell Publishing Group, 1994)

Tanenbaum, Leora, *Catfight: Rivalries Among Women* (Harper Paperbacks, 2003)

Tieger, Paul D. & Barron, Barbara, *Do What You Are* (Sphere, 2007)

Tolle, Eckhart, *The Power of Now: A Guide to Spiritual Enlightenment* (Mobius, 2005)

Wiersbe, Warren, *Be What You Are* (SP Trust, 1989)

Kasey Edwards has no astounding achievements that she can list self-deprecatingly in her bio. She has not written a previous bestseller, did not tread the boards to critical acclaim in her youth, and the closest she's come to doing aid work in Africa is her annual donation to World Vision.

She lives a fairly ordinary life with her partner Chris and dog Toffee, and is flattered beyond belief that you have read her book.

✳